Volume 1

THE COMPLETE ENCYCLOPEDIA OF
CRAFTS

© Marshall Cavendish Limited, 1975
Distributed by Columbia House, 51 West 52nd Street, New York, New York 10019
Printed in U. S. A.

COLUMBIA HOUSE/New York

THE COMPLETE ENCYCLOPEDIA OF
CRAFTS

PAPER

Paper is an exciting, flexible material which can be cut, folded and shaped for hundreds of creative and decorative uses. You can turn it into animated greeting cards, bind books, make pictures or silhouettes, Christmas decorations (expensive to buy!), mobiles, lamp shades, flowers, puppets. Paper is relatively cheap and working with it appeals to all age groups. Art shops stock paper in colours and qualities to inspire the craftsman.

Pop-up cards are easy once you've mastered a few basic techniques. Find the heart card on page 58.

Paper flowers—start with tissue paper on page 86. For the more ambitious volume 2 shows how with crêpe paper.

A beautifully wrapped and decorated gift says so much more. Learn the art yourself in volume 3.

YARN

Yarn becomes cloth by the process of knitting, crochet, weaving, macramé. It can be thin as gossamer or thick as rope, smooth as silk or gnarled and textured like knop-woven wool. It can be plaited, braided, twisted into tassels or ropes; used to decorate a surface as in collage, embroidery and needlepoint. It can be combined with cloth to make rya rugs and there's great scope for combining different methods—weaving a shawl and trimming it with a macramé fringe.

Weaving—begin with finger weaving before going on to simple loom techniques using a picture frame.

Pictorial tapestry (above) is weaving 'proper'. This is not so daunting a step as you'll discover in volume 4.

Embroidery starts in volume 3 and covers all the main traditional stitches plus many fashion ideas for you to try.

CLAY

The word clay is used here to cover a variety of modelling materials including real clay, clays with self-hardening additives and plaster of paris. The main consideration with real clay is that you need a kiln which is expensive to buy, so we suggest some ways to get around the problem. Meanwhile you can learn in the first half dozen chapters how the basic ways of handling clay can be used with self-hardening clays.

The block—one of the simplest shapes– that can be made of clay. These clay dice are both decorative and useful. See page 60.

Later volumes show how with real clay. Plus a valuable section on how to repair china, pottery and porcelain.

PLASTIC

Plastic, the material of the future, is still little used by many craftsmen. It can be worked into a wide range of beautiful objects and comes in hard or soft sheets or resin form. Learn to make unusual and elegant items such as paper weights, chess pieces and panels. The interesting challenge is to develop truly 'plastic' objects, rather than copying materials like ivory, because plastic has its own definite character.

The Encyclopedia of Crafts is all about . . .
Relaxation—working on a craft is the best way to forget day-to-day stresses . . . **Pleasure**—the sheer delight of handling beautiful materials and textures . . . **Satisfaction**—making well-made decorative objects much more cheaply than mass manufactured articles . . . **Creativity**—watch your creative skills develop in the months ahead . . . **Fun**—hours spent making things with friends or family are even more fun . . . **Saving money**—many crafts cost you no more than your time and enrich your life and home . . . **Reward**—at the end of the day you have something to show for your effort.

Now you can turn your hand to anything:
This is the first fully illustrated, comprehensive encyclopedia of traditional and modern home crafts. Your permanent reference library of techniques . . . a golden treasury of exciting ideas. Learn step by step all the better-known and some of the lesser known crafts, with easy to follow instructions and photographs. The next few pages give you only a glimpse of some of the many things that you will learn to do, and want to make, in the months ahead. ENCYCLOPEDIA OF CRAFTS introduces you to **hundreds** of things to do and **thousands** of exciting things to make.

METAL

Metal chapters show how to turn wire—brass, copper or silver—into intricate jewelry with nothing more complicated than a pair of pliers. Tin cans become candle covers and Christmas tree decorations, horse shoe nails are changed to pendants and sculptures. Lightweight modern tools make it also possible to solder, weld, beat, cut, cast, and etch at home . . . to make jewelry, dishes, buckles, bowls, plaques and sculptures. They'll be difficult to resist trying.

Horseshoe nail necklaces—chunky jewelry so easy to make for personal pleasure. Page 73 gives step-by-step instructions.

These rings can be made with one or two coils of wire around the finger. So simple—so attractive (see page 127).

Nails are usually taken for granted but this panel shows that a good selection can make a brilliant design (see page 688).

Knitting and crochet—we take beginners through the first steps then introduce fresh ideas to the old familiar techniques.

Catherine wheel motifs—just keep on working until they're the required size. Versatile round motifs page 152.

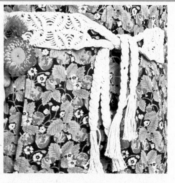

Knotting makes use of anything from silk to string. The series starts in volume 2 with Macramé Made Easy.

Yarn has boundless possibilities and ingenious craftsmen continually interpret and update old techniques. **Needlepoint** starts with straight stitches; then shows a variety of stitches and patterns specially designed for you by Tapestry Bazaar and the Pearson Gorman Needlepoint School. In **tatting** and **bobbin lace** there are the traditional methods and patterns plus very exciting modern works. Going through a popular revival at the moment is **rug-making**—including hooked rugs, Rya rugs and oriental methods. Also valuable information on mending and restoring of rugs.

These are examples of clear cast embedding which is described on page 32. The first of many ideas with plastic.

Bring back memories of the seashore with a resin and embedded shell tile. See volume 6.

ENAMEL

Enamelling is the craft of applying glass powder to metal surfaces and heating in a small kiln until the glass melts and fuses. You can make enamelled jewelry either pop or elegant, brilliant buttons, shiny buckles, dishes, tiles, front door numbers, box lids. We show how to handle glass millefiore, foiling cloisonné and pliqué-au-jour. Small kilns now make home enamelling practical—so it's in for a big revival.

The brilliant colours created by enamelling even the simplest pieces make this a fascinating craft for you to try.

CLOTH

The cloth section is concerned with all aspects of combining and joining pieces of cloth—from satins and velvets to cheesecloth, denim and tweeds. It divides into nine main areas—sewing clothes and home furnishings, fabric collage, soft sculpture, patchwork, applique, soft toys, quilting, upholstery and millinery. We show you how to use the right cloth, achieve the right 'cut' and put the work together correctly in a fast, simple and creative way.

Sewing to wear—styles are simply constructed so that sewing is foolproof. Beautiful clothes to make, fashionable to wear.

Sewing for the home—new curtains or quilts don't break the budget if you make them yourself. Start now—page 70.

Soft sculpture is a term loosely applied to all sorts of sewn and stuffed objects—more fun than a serious art form.

COLOUR

The main thing about colour is that you don't have to be 'artistic' to use it successfully. Using colour is the most effective way to change or revive a surface. There are colour sections on **painting, dyeing** and **printing**—and wherever there is a surface, you can colour it brighter and more beautifully. Learn dozens of craft techniques that give stunning results once you see how the experts do it—and the methods are easy once you get the knack.

Printing starts on page 76 with simple fruit shapes. Later chapters cover a host of techniques including Letraset and type.

Stencils provide you with a method of putting colour exactly where you want it, even if you can't draw a straight line!

Dyeing—fabric dyes, layer dyeing, bleach line work, free hand dye painting and tie-dyeing. Begins in volume 2.

WOOD

Presenting the four main subjects from a woman's point of view—carpentry, finishes, renovation and sculpting. Working with wood does not depend on biceps any longer since everyone can use power tools to make anything from shelves to sculpture. Or you can begin with furniture finishes and learn all about polyurethane coating, varnishes, waxes and stains. It's all money-saving and well worth a few leisure hours.

Basic carpentry—not just facts but also how to apply them to make a wide range of useful projects. Starts at page 18.

Decorative carpentry. An acquired skill but start with a coping saw and discover how easy it is to cut curves. . . .

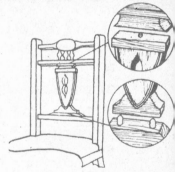
Sculpting deals with a wide range of creative ideas. Start you carving and whittling with volume 3.

DESIGN

Design know-how provides a refresher course in simple geometry and discusses and explains colour effects, schemes, texture, pattern and symmetry. You can refer to the chapters on proportion when making a clay pot and the collection of trace patterns helps you with your paper pictures, needlepoint and embroidery designs.

Example from **Motif Collection**

PLUS

Other sections included are **Beadwork,** with instructions on mending and restyling old necklaces, **Lapidary**—how to find, identify, tumble, polish and cut stones. **Basketry** takes a beautiful old craft and adapts it to today's needs. There's also **mobiles, mosaics, kite-making, fur, leather, kitchencrafts, egg decorating** and **home herbalist.** There are several sections on using materials from nature-feather flowers, corn dollies, seeds for jewelry and more.

Mobiles to make (page 110)

Toys—the delight of a child with your pleasure in making them yourself. Start with a big bad bean bag mouse.

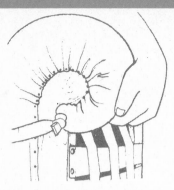

Upholstery teaches you how to remake old furniture for a fraction of the new cost. From volume 4.

Applique, patchwork and collage are three crafts that began in thrift and flourish as art. Add to your family heirlooms.

This child's sun hat is just one of the many ideas in **millinery.** Make one for yourself as well (page 624).

Gilding—for picture frames, jewelry boxes and restoring gilt on period furniture. Learn to use delicate gold leaf.

GLASS

We all use glass objects every day—but how many people have tried to work with glass? Certainly, skilled craftsmen devote years to study; but nowadays you don't need elaborate training to create pretty effects on ordinary glassware. And, with practice, you can use sophisticated techniques of cutting and staining with your own designs. Glass is a beautiful, rewarding material and you will discover dozens of ways to use it.

By using stencils and a mild safe etching fluid you can even etch labels on jars. Simple and effective—see page 142.

An attractive lampshade— made quite simply from a glass carboy or demi-john bottle. Details in volume 5.

WAX

Wax deals with all kinds of decorative and perfumed candle-making and wax modelling. Make evening garden parties glow with flares, stabbed firmly into the grass or earth. They are made by building up a candle on a wick by pouring molten wax down the wick— the same process used for making long church candles. For the more ambitious try sand candles with their attractive biscuit-like crusts (see page 82).

Make your own beautiful candles using the instructive guide to dipping, carving, twisting and plaiting candles. (Page 52.)

CREATIVE IDEAS

Creative ideas are small, quick things to make—crafty ideas for gifts or bazaar items such as mobiles, decorating denim with studs, pompoms, toys, Scandinavian wall stars, buckles from brass hinges, and sequin necklaces.
In volume 2 we re-vamp everyday objects with mirror mosaic tiles to create the most unusual place mats, cigarette tin, vase and bracelet you've ever seen.

Ideas for soak-on transfers brighten up your desk with colourful pencils, pots and mugs (turn to page 57).

Leather (in volume 2)

Flowers and plants (volume 5)

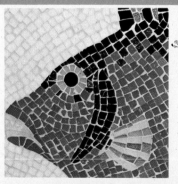

Mosaics (starts volume 4)

Basketry (starts volume 2)

Contents

✱ **Not suitable for children without adult supervision.**

ADDRESSES OF MAIL ORDER SUPPLIERS

ARTS & CRAFTS, GENERAL
California
Gemex Co.
900 W. Los Vallecitos Boulevard
San Marcos, California 92069

Illinois
Lee Wards
Creative Crafts Center
1200 St. Charles Street
Elgin, Illinois 60120

Triarco Arts & Crafts
P. O. Box 106
Northfield, Illinois 60093

Massachusetts
Earth Guild
15 P. Tudor Street
Cambridge, Massachusetts 02139

Missouri
Skil-Crafts
305 Virginia Avenue
Joplin, Missouri 64801

Nebraska
Mangelsen's
8200 J Street
Omaha, Nebraska 68127

New York
Arthur Brown
2 West 46th Street
New York, New York 10036

Craft Service
337 University Avenue
Rochester, New York 14607

Economy Handicrafts
47-11 Francis Lewis Boulevard
Flushing, New York 11361

Texas
American Handicrafts
8113 Highway 80 West
Fort Worth, Texas 76116

Wisconsin
Sax Art and Crafts
207 N. Milwaukee St.
Milwaukee, Wisconsin 53202

BASKETRY
Connecticut
H. H. Perkins
10 S. Bradley Road
Woodbridge, Connecticut 06525

Illinois
Dick Blick Co.
P. O. Box 1267
Galesburg, Illinois 61401

New York
Ace Rattan Products
60-19 54th Place
Maspeth, New York 11378

BATIK
Michigan
Polyproducts Corp.
13810 Nelson Avenue
Detroit, Michigan 48227

New York
Utrecht Linens
33 35th Street
Brooklyn, New York 11232

BEADS
California
The Bead Game
8071 Beverly Boulevard
Los Angeles, California 90048

New York
Grey Owl Indian Mfg. Co., Inc.
150-02 Beaver Road
Jamaica, New York 11433

South Dakota
Del Trading Post
P. O. Box 248
Mission, South Dakota 57555

BOTTLE-CUTTING
New York
Avalon Industries, Inc.
200 Fifth Avenue
New York, New York 10010

CANDLE-MAKING
California
Gemex Co.
900 West Los Vallecitos Boulevard
San Marcos, California 92069

General Supplies Co.
526 Aviation Road
Fallbrook, California 92028

Sippewisset Wax Works
Box 453
Seaside, California 93955

Florida
Island Crafts
5735 14th Street W.
Bradenton, Florida 33507

Illinois
Triarco Arts & Crafts
P. O. Box 106
Northfield, Illinois 60093

Massachusetts
International Candle House
349 Congress Street
Boston, Massachusetts 02210

K.R. Ruckstuhl, Inc.
P. O. Box 663
Provincetown, Massachusetts 02657

Missouri
Skil-Crafts
305 Virginia Avenue
Joplin, Missouri 64801

Nebraska
Mangelsen's
8200 J Street
Omaha, Nebraska 68127

New Jersey
A. I. Root
1106 East Grand Street
Elizabeth, New Jersey 07201

New York
Economy Handicrafts
47-11 Francis Lewis Boulevard
Flushing, New York 11361

Pennsylvania
George Arold
P. O. Box 99
Hatfield, Pennsylvania 19440

Texas
American Handicrafts
P. O. Box 791
Fort Worth, Texas 76101

Washington
Barker Enterprises
15106—10th Avenue S. W.
Seattle, Washington 98166

Pourette Mfg. Co.
6818 Roosevelt Way, N. E.
Seattle, Washington 98115

Wisconsin
Sax Arts and Crafts
201 N. Milwaukee St.
Milwaukee, Wisconsin 53202

CANING AND RUSHING
California
The Caning Shop
1279 Gilman Street
Berkeley, California 94704

Naturalcraft
2199 Bancroft Way
Berkeley, California 94704

Connecticut
H. H. Perkins
10 S. Bradley Road
Woodbridge, Connecticut 06525

Illinois
Dick Blick Co.
P. O. Box 1267
Galesburg, Illinois 61401

New York
Alnap Co., Inc.
66 Reade Street
New York, New York 10007

**CERAMICS MATERIALS
AND CLAY**
Indiana
American Art Clay Co., Inc.
4717 West 16th Street
Indianapolis, Indiana 46222

New York
Long Island Ceramic Center
1190 Route 109
Lindenhurst, New York 11757

DECOUPAGE
Illinois
Dick Blick
P. O. Box 1267
Galesburg, Illinois 61401

Missouri
Skil-Crafts
β05 Virginia Avenue
Joplin, Missouri 64801

New York
Economy Handicrafts
47-11 Francis Lewis Boulevard
Flushing, New York 11361

Texas
American Handicrafts
P. O. Box 791
Fort Worth, Texas 76101

DYES
Alabama
Owl and Olive Weavers
704 29th Street South
Birmingham, Alabama 35233

California
The Mercantile
P. O. Box 343
Berkeley, California 94701

Kansas
The Yarn Barn
Box 334
730 Massachusetts
Lawrence, Kansas 66044

Massachusetts
Earth Guild/Grateful Union
15 Tudor Street
Cambridge, Massachusetts 02139

Minnesota
The Yarnery
1648 Grand Avenue
St. Paul, Minnesota 55105

New Mexico
Village Wools Fibercraft Materials
and Supplies
308 San Felipe, N. W.
Albuquerque, New Mexico 87104

Oregon
Wildflower Fibers
211 N. W. Davis Street
Portland, Oregon 97209

Pennsylvania
Lenos Handcrafts
2037 Walnut Street
Philadelphia, Pennsylvania 19103

Texas
Craft Industries
1513 West Alabama
Houston, Texas 77006

Utah
Intertwine
217 Trolley Square
Salt Lake City, Utah 84102

**ENAMELS AND
ENAMELLING MATERIALS**
California
Seaire
17909 South Hobart Boulevard
Gardena, California 90248

Illinois
Thomas C. Thompson Co.
Highland Park, Illinois 60035

Missouri
Skil-Crafts
305 Virginia Avenue
Joplin, Missouri 64801

New York
Allcraft Tool & Supply Co.
215 Park Avenue
Hicksville, New York 11801

Economy Handicrafts
47-11 Francis Lewis Boulevard
Flushing, New York 11361

Texas
American Handicrafts
P. O. Box 791
Fort Worth, Texas 76101

**FLOWER-MAKING
MATERIALS**
New York
S. Beckenstein, Inc.
130 Orchard Street
New York, New York 10022

GLASS (STAINED)
Arizona
Art Glass of Arizona, Inc.
2047 North 16th Street
Phoenix, Arizona 85006

California
Augustine Glass Works
929-B Pico Boulevard
Santa Monica, California 90405

Glass by Humber
700 Filbert Street
San Francisco, California 94133

Nervo Art Stained Glass Works
4911 Telegraph Avenue
Oakland, California 94609

Illinois
Acme Glass Co.
2215 West Roosevelt Road
Chicago, Illinois 60608

Maryland
CCM Arts and Crafts, Inc.
9520 Baltimore Avenue
College Park, Maryland 20740

Massachusetts
Stained Glass of Hanover
Box 3065
Hanover, Massachusetts 02339

Whittemore-Durgin Glass Co.
Box 2065 AB
Hanover, Massachusetts 02339

Whittemore-Durgin Glass Co.
825 Market Street
Rockland, Massachusetts 02370

New Jersey
Glass Work Bench
159 Main Street
Flemington, New Jersey 08822

Stancraft
2005 Highway 35
Oakhurst, New Jersey 07755

New York
Allcraft Tool & Supply Co.
215 Park Avenue
Hicksville, New York 11801

S. A. Bendheim Co., Inc.
122 Hudson Street
New York, New York 10013

Economy Handicrafts
47-11 Francis Lewis Boulevard
Flushing, New York 11361

Glass Masters Guild
52 Carmine Street
New York, New York 10014

Ohio
Franklin Art Glass Studios
222 East Sycamore Street
Columbus, Ohio 43206

Pennsylvania
Willet Stained Glass Studios
10 E. Moreland Avenue
Philadelphia, Pennsylvania 19118

Texas
American Handicrafts
P. O. Box 791
Fort Worth, Texas 76101

Virginia
Arts & Crafts Studio
7221 Little River Turnpike
Annandale, Virginia 22003

Washington
Alpha Faceting Supply
Box 2133, Dept. C
Bremerton, Washington 98310

Stained Glass Studio
12519 Lake City Way N. E.
Seattle, Washington 98125

ADDRESSES OF MAIL ORDER SUPPLIERS

**JEWELRY FINDINGS
AND MATERIALS**

California
California Crafts Supply
1419 North Central Park Avenue
Anaheim, California 92802

Gemex Co.
900 W. Los Vallecitos Blvd.
San Marcos, California 92069

Jewelart, Inc.
7753 Densmore Avenue
Van Nuys, California 91406

Illinois
Dick Blick
P. O. Box 1267
Galesburg, Illinois 61401

Triarco Arts & Crafts
P. O. Box 106
Northfield, Illinois 60093

Maryland
CCM Arts and Crafts, Inc.
9520 Baltimore Avenue
College Park, Maryland 20740

Michigan
C. R. Hill Co.
35 W. Grand River Avenue
Detroit, Michigan 48226

New York
Allcraft Tool & Supply Co., Inc.
22 West 48th Street
New York, New York 10020

Economy Handicrafts
47-11 Francis Lewis Boulevard
Flushing, New York 11361

Magic Novelty Co., Inc.
95 Morton Street
New York, New York 10014

Vanguard Crafts Inc.
2915 Avenue J
Brooklyn, N.Y. 11210

Ohio
Kraft Korner
5864 Mayfield Road
Cleveland, Ohio 44124

National Artcrafts Supply Co.
12217 Euclid Avenue
Cleveland, Ohio 44160

Wisconsin
Nasco House of Crafts
901 Janesville Avenue
Ft. Atkinson, Wisconsin 53538

Sax Arts and Crafts
207 N. Milwaukee Street
Milwaukee, Wisconsin 53202

KNOTTING AND WEAVING

New Jersey
Boin Arts and Crafts
91 Morris Street
Morristown, New Jersey 07960

New York
P. C. Herwig Co., Inc.
264 Clinton Street
Brooklyn, New York 11201

LEATHERCRAFT

California
California Crafts Supply
1096 North Main Street
Orange, California 92667

Connecticut
S & S Art and Crafts
Colchester, Connecticut 06415

Illinois
Triarco Arts & Crafts
P. O. Box 106
Northfield, Illinois 60093

Massachusetts
Berman Leather
147 S Street
Boston, Massachusetts 02111

Missouri
The Brown Leather Co.
305 Virginia Avenue
Joplin, Missouri 64801

Skil-Crafts
305 Virginia Avenue
Joplin, Missouri 64801

New York
Art Handicrafts Co.
3512 Flatlands Avenue
Brooklyn, New York 11234

Economy Handicrafts
47-11 Francis Lewis Boulevard
Flushing, New York 11361

P. C. Herwig Co., Inc.
264 Clinton Street
Brooklyn, New York 11201

Leathercrafters Supply Co.
25 Great Jones Street
New York, New York 10012

Tandy Leather Co.
330 Fifth Avenue
New York, New York 10018

Wisconsin
Sax Arts and Crafts
207 North Milwaukee Street
Milwaukee, Wisconsin 53202

METALCRAFTING

Illinois
Apollo Metals, Inc.
6650 Oak Park Avenue
Chicago, Illinois 60638

Maryland
CCM Arts and Crafts, Inc.
9520 Baltimore Avenue
College Park, Maryland 20740

New York
Allcraft Tool & Supply Co.
215 Park Avenue
Hicksville, New York 11801

MOSAICS

Illinois
Dick Blick
P. O. Box 1267
Galesburg, Illinois 61401

New York
Economy Handicrafts
47-11 Francis Lewis Boulevard
Flushing, New York 11361

Soriano Ceramics
2021 Steinway Street
Long Island City, New York 11106

NEEDLECRAFTS

California
Gemex Co.
900 W. Los Vallecitos Boulevard
San Marcos, California 92069

Naturalcraft
2199 Bancroft Way
Berkeley, California 94704

Illinois
Lee Wards
1200 St. Charles Street
Elgin, Illinois 60120

New York
Bell Yarn
75 Essex Street
New York, New York 10002

Economy Handicrafts
47-11 Francis Lewis Boulevard
Flushing, New York 11361

Goldman's Yarn Stores, Inc.
4417 13th Avenue
Brooklyn, New York 11219

Alice Maynard
724 Fifth Avenue
New York, New York 10019

Texas
Merribee Needlecraft Co.
2904 W. Lancaster
Ft. Worth, Texas 76107

**PAPERCRAFTS AND
PAPIER-MÂCHÉ**

Connecticut
S & S Art and Crafts
Colchester, Connecticut 06415

Illinois
Dick Blick
P. O. Box 1267
Galesburg, Illinois 61401

Triarco Arts & Crafts
P. O. Box 106
Northfield, Illinois 60093

Maryland
CCM Arts & Crafts, Inc.
9520 Baltimore Avenue
College Park, Maryland 20740

Missouri
Skil-Crafts
305 Virginia Avenue
Joplin, Missouri 64801

New York
Economy Handicrafts
47-11 Francis Lewis Boulevard
Flushing, New York 11361

Wisconsin
Nasco House of Crafts
901 Janesville Avenue
Ft. Atkinson, Wisconsin 53538

Sax Arts and Crafts
207 N. Milwaukee Street
Milwaukee, Wisconsin 53202

PLASTICS

California
Cadillac Plastic & Chemical Co.
11255 Vanowen
North Hollywood, California 91605

Georgia
Cadillac Plastic & Chemical Co.
1500 Carroll Drive, N. W.
Atlanta, Georgia 30318

Illinois
Cadillac Plastic & Chemical Co.
1245 West Fulton
Chicago, Illinois 60607

Maine
Soule Glass and Paint Co.
127 Marginal Way
Portland, Maine 04101

Maryland
CCM Arts & Crafts, Inc.
9520 Baltimore Avenue
College Park, Maryland 20740

Massachusetts
Cadillac Plastic & Chemical Co.
269 McGarth Highway
Boston, Massachusetts 02143

Michigan
Cadillac Plastic & Chemical Co.
15111 Second Avenue
Detroit, Michigan 48203

Polyproducts Corp.
13810 Nelson Avenue
Detroit, Michigan 48227

New Jersey
Cadillac Plastic & Chemical Co.
6025 Colonial Highway
Pennsauken, New Jersey 08109

Smooth-On Corp.
1000 Valley Road
Gillette, New Jersey 07933

New York
Cadillac Plastic & Chemical Co.
35-21 Vernon Boulevard
Long Island City, New York 11106

Industrial Plastic
309 Canal Street
New York, New York 10013

The Plastics Factory
119 Avenue D
New York, New York 10009

Ohio
Cadillac Plastic & Chemical Co.
3818 Red Bank Road
Cincinnati, Ohio 45227

Texas
Cadillac Plastic & Chemical Co.
2546 Irving Boulevard
Dallas, Texas 75207

ROCK POLISHING

California
Great Western Equipment Co.
3444 Main Street
Chula Vista, California 92011

New Jersey
Craftools Inc.
1 Industrial Road
Wood Ridge, New Jersey 07075

Triarco Arts & Crafts
P. O. Box 106
Northfield, Illinois 60093

Maryland
CCM Arts & Crafts, Inc.
9520 Baltimore Avenue
College Park, Maryland 20740

Missouri
Skil-Crafts
305 Virginia Avenue
Joplin, Missouri 64801

New York
Economy Handicrafts
47-11 Francis Lewis Boulevard
Flushing, New York 11361

Wisconsin
Nasco House of Crafts
901 Janesville Avenue
Ft. Atkinson, Wisconsin 53538

Sax Arts and Crafts
207 N. Milwaukee Street
Milwaukee, Wisconsin 53202

Ohio
National Artcraft Supply Co.
12217 Euclid Avenue
Cleveland, Ohio 44160

Wisconsin
Sax Arts and Crafts
207 N. Milwaukee Street
Milwaukee, Wisconsin 53202

SILKSCREEN

New York
Arthur Brown, Inc.
2 West 46th Street
New York, New York 10036

STONE GRINDING

California
Felker Manufacturing Co.
1900-F So. Crenshaw Boulevard
Torrance, California 90501

Walter E. Johansen
P. O. Box 907
Morgan Hill, California 95037

Indiana
Gemstone Shop
17561 State Road 23 N. E.
South Bend, Indiana 46635

Texas
Gem Center, U.S.A.
4100 Alameda
El Paso, Texas 79905

WIRECRAFTING

Illinois
Dick Blick
P. O. Box 1267
Galesburg, Illinois 61401

Maryland
CCM Arts & Crafts, Inc.
9520 Baltimore Avenue
College Park, Maryland 20740

Missouri
Skil-Crafts
305 Virginia Avenue
Joplin, Missouri 64801

New York
Allcraft Tool and Supply Co.
215 Park Avenue
Hicksville, New York 11801

Economy Handicrafts
47-11 Francis Lewis Boulevard
Flushing, New York 11361

WOODFINDINGS

Maine
Saunders Brothers
Westbrook, Maine 04092

New York
Duplex Novelty Co.
315 West 35th Street
New York, New York 10001

YARN

California
The Yarn Depot, Inc.
545 Sutter Street
San Francisco, California 94102

Connecticut
Cottage Crafts
Pomfret Center, Connecticut 06259

Minnesota
The Yarnery
1648 Grand Avenue
St. Paul Minnesota 55105

New York
Economy Handicrafts
47-11 Francis Lewis Boulevard
Flushing, New York 11361

Home Yarn Co.
1849 Coney Island Avenue
Brooklyn, New York 11230

Paternayan Bros., Inc.
312 E. 95 Street
New York, New York 10028

Ohio
Colonial Woolen Mills, Inc.
6501 Barberton Avenue
Cleveland, Ohio 44102

Oregon
Oregon Worsted Co.
8300 S. E. McLaughlin Boulevard
Portland, Oregon 97202

Pennsylvania
Walter McCook & Son, Inc.
31 No. 10th Street
Philadelphia, Pennsylvania 19107

First fold your paper...

Choosing the materials

It is important to select the right paper to work with. Paper that is too thin and floppy will not fold or stand satisfactorily, whereas thin cardboard is difficult to manipulate, and if it is coated the surface may crack. To begin with, use a good quality uncoated paper such as construction paper, available in a wide variety of colors from art shops.

The slit principle

The simplest pop-up construction is made by cutting a single horizontal slit across a vertical fold in a piece of paper. This makes a basic opening inside which an eye, a message or a motif can be centered. Or it can form a beak or mouth as illustrated in the completed bird and fish cards.

Bright, original pop-up cards are easy to make and can be elaborated upon once you get the knack of a few basic techniques. The cards work on the principle of a cut made across a fold in the paper. This frees a section of the paper which is then folded to give a 3-dimensional pop-up that opens and closes to look like a winking eye, a talking mouth, or a quacking beak.

The basic construction is simply the slit and the fold, but a wide variety of original effects can be achieved by adding to this simple technique.

Constructing the pop-up. It is a good idea to experiment with lined paper to begin with, so that the creases can be made accurately.

Fold the paper in half twice to make the card shape (fig.1). Open up the card and fold the inside crease in the opposite direction. Snip horizontally through the crease not more than half way across (fig.2). Fold back the edges of the slit to make two right angled triangles (fig.3). Turn the paper over and fold these triangles over the other way (fig.4). Repeat once or twice more to make the fold workable.

Open up the card flat (fig.5). With the left thumb holding down the top crease, use the right forefinger to lift the pop-up (fig.6). Press pop-up crease firmly (fig.7). Repeat with the other half of the pop-up. Carefully shut the card, if necessary helping the pop-up outwards, and keeping the top and bottom creases folding with the centre fold of the card. Press the closed card flat firmly with the knuckles.

Open and shut the card several times until it suggests a picture idea. If it reminds you of a duck you could add the face to match and write QUACK! inside the beak. If it looks like a baby bird, how about adding a worm dangling from the beak?

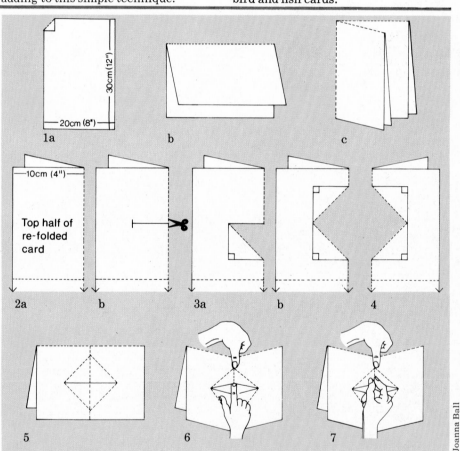

Joanna Ball

Decorating the cards

Use a variety of colored stick-ons, gummed paper or paints to finish the design on your card.

For example, trace body shapes, plants and flowers from illustrations, cut out in colored paper and stick them to the card. Experiment to find the different effects you can achieve by applying various finishes to the same basic pop-up—like the 3 cards illustrated here.

The frog card with the winking eye and moving butterfly shape is a more sophisticated development of the basic technique described here.

To make the bird card
You will need:
Red construction paper measuring 19cm x 30cm (8″ x 12″)
Green paper measuring 15cm (6″) square
Scraps of orange and yellow gummed paper, or orange and yellow crayons
Gummed reinforcements
Scissors, glue

☐ Fold the red paper and make a 6.5cm (2½″) wide slit. Draw around a cup to give a circular body shape and around 3 small coins to give the tail.

☐ Cut out the bird shape in green paper. Trace and cut out the diamond beak shape from the green body.

Steve Bicknell

☐ Stick the body onto the card so that the diamond cut-out lies exactly over the pop-up shape.

☐ Either color in the beak shape, or use an orange paper beak shape, cut in half horizontally and stuck onto each half of the pop-up.

☐ Draw on the wing shapes and stick on gummed reinforcements for eyes, with inked pupils in the center. Complete the card by sticking on feet and legs cut from bright yellow gummed paper, or draw them in yellow crayon

To make the fish card

You will need:

Blue construction paper measuring 19cm x 30cm (8″ x 12″)

Green paper measuring 15cm (6″) square

Scraps of dark green, white, yellow and black gummed paper, or crayons in the same colors

Scissors, glue

☐ Fold the blue paper and make a 5cm (2″) wide slit. The mouth shape is varied here as the top and bottom 'lip' are different sizes. This is simply done by folding back the triangles to different depths (fig.8). If the upper triangle is smaller, this gives a small upper lip and a deeper lower lip (fig.9).

☐ Draw the large fish shape (fig.10) and cut out from the green paper. Make a slit for the mouth. Stick the fish onto the card.

☐ Finish off with fins and scales in the dark green paper, a group of white bubbles and circular yellow eyes. Make the pupils from circles of black paper with a triangle snipped out.

☐ Inside the pop-up, stick a square of white paper to the back of the card to look like a throat.

☐ Trace the tiny fish (fig.11) and cut from green paper. Stick in place.

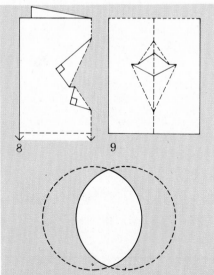

8   9

10. *Use small plates to draw the big fish.*

11. *Tracing pattern for the tiny fish.*

Above: a cheerful robin card based on the simplest pop-up construction, which lends itself particularly well to the gaping bird beak shape.

Below: here the pop-up is shaped like a fish mouth with a shorter upper 'lip'. A tiny fish inside the mouth and a trail of bubbles completes it.

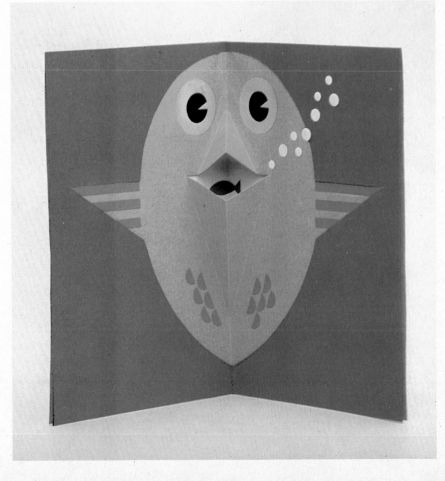

Getting the feel of clay

4

Clay is one of the most satisfying materials to work with. Even simple pinching and modeling with your fingers can produce exciting results and is a good way of becoming familiar with the texture and properties of clay. You can start working in a basic way without a kiln and, if your imagination is stimulated, then go on to use a potter's wheel and fire your own designs.

Natural clay. A lump of clay is made up of millions of tiny, plate-shaped particles. Water enables these flat particles to slide over each other without breaking up. When clay is dry, the particles will not move and if forced, will break. When only a small amount of water is present, movement is limited, and the clay is stiff to use.

When the clay is about 25% water it can be easily molded and is ideal for modeling. More water turns the clay into a soft, formless mass.

Natural clay has the great advantage for the beginner of being an extremely cheap material. Two types of clay are commercially available: white clay is smooth, takes glaze well and is cleaner to use, whereas terracotta clay fires to a pleasant red color at a fairly low temperature. Ready-to-use clay is avail-

As the clay chapters progress you will discover how to use a potter's wheel to make pots and pitchers, how to make vases using the slab technique, use beautiful glazes and slips, and model both life-like and stylized animals and birds. The pitcher shown here is made by Alan Caiger-Smith, the slab vase by Joan Hepworth, oval vase by Mary White, eggcup by David Leach and bird by Stanislas Reychan.

able by mail direct from the manufacturers, and usually contains about 25% water. It is wrapped in plastic bags of various sizes, the 25kg (55lbs) weight being the most convenient for beginners. Store it in a cool place, carefully wrapped in plastic so that it does not dry out. When you have molded the clay into a finished pot or model, the dried clay can be turned into a hard, permanent material by firing it in a pottery oven or kiln, a sawdust pit, or even a bonfire.

Self-hardening clays. For potters who do not have kilns, specially compounded clay mixtures are now available which, when exposed to the air for about 24-48 hours, become really hard and should not break or scratch. The self-hardening clays are clean to use, but are less satisfying to handle than natural clay. They are widely available from hobby shops, but are relatively expensive.

Pots made from self-hardening clay are not entirely durable, they cannot be glazed and they do not hold water. If you varnish them thoroughly first however, they can be made waterproof. Manufacturers supply varnishes intended for use with their clay products, and these can be applied over painted decorations. Some of the self-hardening clays can be fired, if you have access to a kiln, so that your most successful pieces can be made impervious.

Some of these commercially manufactured products have an added advantage in that they are natural potting clay containing a hardening additive, rather than a synthetic substitute, so they handle like natural clay.

Handling qualities. Test the properties of your own clay; dry some pieces

out and see how hard they become, wet other pieces and see how the amount of water present affects this quality of the clay, which is called plasticity. Pinching the clay and working it with a little water will quickly mix the two. A good test for judging the working qualities of the clay is to roll a piece between your hand into a coil which

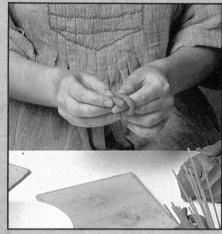

Testing the quality of the clay.

you wrap around your finger. If the coil bends without breaking, does not stick to your finger and retains its shape, then it is probably just right. If it cracks, it is too dry, and if it sticks and is floppy, it is too wet.

Decorating unfired clay. If you are planning to work a design on the clay, press interesting shapes with snap fasteners, tiny buttons, or a pen-knife against the clay before it hardens.

Paint the clay only when it is completely dry. Several types of paint are useful for decorating. Poster paint used direct from the pot gives a strong opaque color. India inks are waterproof and dry to give a semi-matt surface and subtle colors. Gouache colors are also excellent for decorating clay. For a shiny, durable finish, on painted patterns use a suitable clear varnish such as paper varnish or polyurethane lacquer.

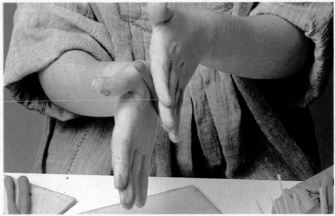

1. Long beads—rolling the clay in the hands.

2. Long beads—rolling the clay with a tile.

3. Long beads—cutting coils.

4. Making the holes.

5. Cutting equal lengths.

6. Round beads–rolling a ball.

7. Pressing a pattern with a knife.

8. Painting beads with poster paint.

9. Varnishing.

10. Completed beads.

11. Threading beads on suede strings.

Making clay beads

Beads and other pieces of jewelry are good first projects to make in clay. They are small and simple to construct, but can be decorated to give impressive finished results.

You will need:

About 340gm (¾lb) clay will make one necklace

Tile or flat piece of wood

Poster paints, India inks or gouache colours

Shapes for impressing

Varnish

Flat working surface, covered with burlap or canvas for natural clay

Smock or apron

Suede strips about 3mm (1/10") wide in suitable lengths for necklaces

Long beads. Roll lengths of clay between your hands (fig.1), then make them perfectly smooth and even by rolling each coil with a flat piece of wood or a ceramic tile (fig.2). Make several coils of the same thickness.

☐Use the knife to cut the coil into lengths – about 12mm-20mm (½"-¾") is a good length, although some could be smaller – rolling the coils as you do so (figs.3,4). This roll-and-slice movement prevents the coil being flattened.

☐Make holes with a thick piece of pointed wire, a needle, or even a piece of spaghetti which has the advantage of not sticking to the clay.

☐Place the beads on newspaper to dry.

Round beads. Roll out even coils of clay, this time making the coils thicker. To get balls the same size, cut equal lengths carefully. To make the balls, roll the cut lengths between the palms of your hands (figs 5,6).

☐Make the holes as before.

Square beads. Roll a coil, then flatten it with a piece of wood if you want to make flat beads, or into a square block for square beads.

☐Cut and pierce as before.

Finishing the pieces. Impress any designs at this stage (fig.7).

When the clay is dry, smooth the surface with a damp sponge. Do not over-sponge, as this will roughen the surface. If you have access to a kiln, the pieces can be fired to a temperature of about 980°–1000°C (1821°–1857°F).

Potters using self-hardening clay should allow the pieces to dry for several days in the air, after which they will become very hard, although this clay can still be softened in water. Thread the beads when they are completely dry on lengths of thick wire or spaghetti and paint them with poster paints or India inks (fig.8). Leave to dry thoroughly and paint with a coat of clear varnish (fig.9).

Clay beads look attractive threaded on narrow suede strips (fig.11), which can be bought from hobby shops, or can be cut from suede scraps using scissors or a sharp blade.

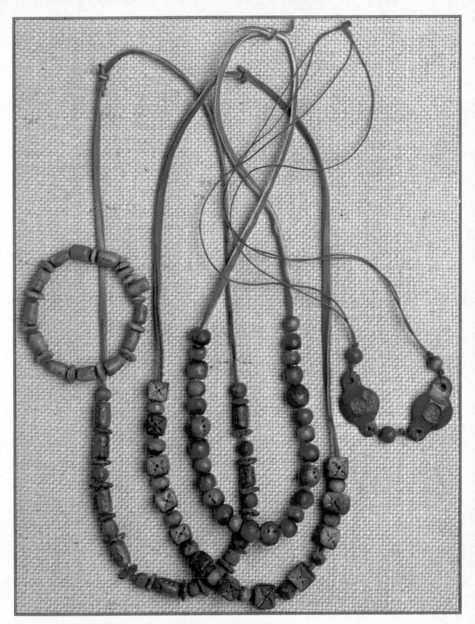

Above: here the beads are a variety of shapes, some with small patterns incised on the surface with a sharp point. Painted in soft shades of green, brown and terracotta and threaded on a narrow suede strip or strong twine, the beads make attractive and original necklaces. Bracelets are best strung on strong elastic thread

Left: pendants provide great scope for making individual patterns, whether they are a simple design, a name, a portrait head or a message. The pendants here show a simple coil, a heart with a design pricked on it and a round pendant with flower shapes stuck onto it. All jewelry by Françoise Theroude.

Designing with straight stitch

Tapestry, canvaswork and needlepoint are all words used to describe the art of building up a solid pattern of yarn on canvas. Usually this is presented as a specific pattern to be made up in a given yarn on a set size of canvas. But with an understanding of what yarns cover what canvas best, you can vary the scale and tailor designs to your own requirements.

You can achieve splendid, rich textures and original designs on canvas, working with any of a variety of yarns. Wool gives a beautifully firm, dense surface which is hardwearing and attractive. With silks and cottons you can work fine, detailed designs, and unusual yarns like raffia and metallic threads create interesting textures.

Canvas. There are 2 types: single thread, measured by the number of threads per 2.5cm (1″) and double thread, measured by the number of pairs of threads per 2.5cm (1″).

Single thread canvas is the best to begin on as you can try out a wide variety of stitches, whereas double thread is restricted to 4 or 5 only. The number of threads per 2.5cm (1″) can vary from 26 for fine work to 3 for very coarse work.

Needles. Use tapestry needles with large eyes and blunt ends. These are available in a variety of sizes, 18-21 being the most popular, but size 14 is better for very coarse canvas.

Yarns are available in many different thicknesses and some are made up of several individual strands twisted together, which can be separated as required. Use a length of yarn about 46cm (18″) long—if it is longer it will wear thin and become fluffy.

Straight stitch is used to work this bag and, as it does not distort the canvas, you don't need a frame. It can be worked over any number of threads, but large stitches are unsuitable for practical designs as they tend to get caught.

Satin stitch is usually worked over 4 threads to give a firm surface, and in this bag it is formed in steps of forward 4 and back 3.

Starting and finishing. Knot one end of the yarn. Put the needle in at the front of the canvas about 5cm (2″) from the position of the first stitch. Bring the needle up from the back and work the first few stitches. Cut off the knot, thread the end into a needle and slip the yarn through the back of the worked stitches, adding a small back stitch to secure. The next length of yarn can be threaded into the back of the previously worked stitches and finished off as before. Avoid fastening on and off in the same place. The extra-thick stitching may show through on the front of the canvas.

Satin stitch clutch bag in rainbow colors, designed and worked by Martyn Thomas.

To make the clutch bag

This neat envelope design is worked entirely in 'stepped' satin stitch blocks using rainbow colors, to create a fishscale effect. The finished bag measures 22.5cm x 15cm (9″ x 6″).

You will need:

Single thread canvas 14 threads per 2.5cm (1″), 50cm x 32cm (22″ x 13″)
Lining fabric, 48cm x 30cm (19″ x 12″)
Choose any yarn suitable for 14 threads per 2.5cm (1″) canvas. Calculate the number of skeins required from the total length of yarn given. Always round out to avoid the risk of running short, since everybody works to a slightly different tension.
Total length of yarn required:
Natural—55m (60yd)
Red—41m (45yd)
Orange—41m (45yd)
Yellow—28m (30yd)
Green—28m (30yd)
Turquoise—28m (30yd)
Blue—14m (15yd)
Violet—14m (15yd)
Tapestry needle No. 18
Snap fastener
Sewing thread and betweens needle for making up

☐ Fold the canvas in half horizontally and vertically to find the center.

Yarn	Length per skein or ball	Canvas size	Needle size
Anchor Tapisserie wool	13.7m (15yd)		
DMC Laine Tapisserie	8m (8.8yd)	14 threads per 2.5cm (1″)	18
Appleton's tapestry wool	13.7m (15yd)		
Appleton's crewel wool (4 strands)	27.5m (30yd)		

☐ Following the design layout (fig.1), begin by working the natural yarn in diagonal lines of satin stitch, starting at the pointed end of the bag, which lies about 5cm (2″) in from the edge of the canvas.

Work the bottom right to top left diagonals in a continuous line. The opposite diagonals break at the intersections, where a small stitch worked over 2 threads fills in at the point where the diagonals cross.

☐ Fill in the colour by following the chart given for the sequence of colours and stitches (fig.2). The filling-in stitches are worked over 2 threads at ends and tip of each color block.

Finishing. Pin the canvas to shape on an ironing board and press gently under a damp cloth. Leave to dry thoroughly. Trim the canvas to within 6 threads of the embroidery.

☐ Miter the center of the bag flap by folding at A and turning under hems B and C (fig.3). Miter other corners, turn under seam allowance and herringbone the canvas to the back of the embroidery.

☐ Cut the lining to size, allowing an extra 1.5cm (½″) all around for turnings. Fold under the seam allowance and baste. Fold the flap lining in the same way as for the mitered canvas.

☐ Slip stitch the lining to the embroidery neatly all around the edge, and overcast the sides of the bag firmly.

☐ Sew the snap fastener to the center of the flap and on bag to correspond.

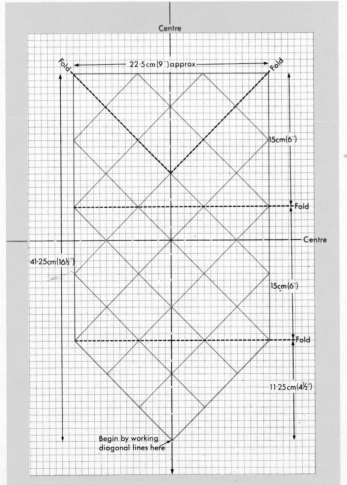

Centre

Fold

22·5cm (9″) approx

Fold

15cm (6″)

Fold

Centre

41·25cm (16½″)

15cm (6″)

Fold

11·25cm (4½″)

Begin by working diagonal lines here

1. Design layout showing the position of the diagonals.

2. Colour and stitch chart, with stitch working detail.

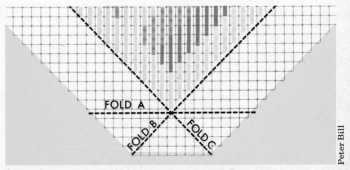

FOLD A

FOLD B

FOLD C

3. Folding the canvas to miter the pointed flap.

Peter Bill

Braiding with scrap materials

Braids are simple enough for children to make, and may have been the first textile process mastered by primitive man. The ancient Egyptians and Peruvians braided fabrics, some as wide as 46cm (18″). Much later, American settlers in New England found it a thrifty way of recycling worn-out clothes. Braiding with scrap material is still an economical and rewarding way of creating fabric. It is a means of producing practical and attractive articles from discarded clothing, scraps of yarn, stockings and panty hose, blankets, curtains and covers using all these materials as a form of yarn. Lap rugs, floor coverings, table mats and cushion covers are just a few of the items that can be made from the contents of a rag bag.

Construction. A braid is formed by interlacing 3 or more strands of yarn just as hair is braided. It is the first step on the road to weaving: later chapters go on to finger weaving which is virtually a form of braiding with numbers of threads. This in turn leads on to building up a warp and weft using rigid heddles and then to working with various types of loom.

Choosing the materials

Bear in mind how you want the finished article to look and what it will be used for. Avoid fabrics that unravel and shed their pile, such as fur fabric, and also scratchy ones that contain metallic threads. Velvets, woolen fabrics and linens tend to fray, so the edges must be turned in carefully to make sure that they don't escape. Felt is useful where a smooth look is wanted as it does not fray but, not being washable, it is unsuitable for items that are likely to get stained. Fluff and dust can be shaken out, or removed by vacuum cleaner. Cotton is suitable for most purposes and is easy and pleasant to braid.

Nylon stockings, panty hose and jersey fabrics are ideal, especially for making cozy and comfortable rugs. Rugs, of course, take a lot of material, so if you are planning a special color scheme you will need whole garments. You can, however, quite successfully blend different types of fabric of toning or contrasting colors, as long as the thickness and weight are the same. When making table mats, choose a washable fabric thick enough to take a hot plate.

Color and design

Completely different effects can be achieved depending on the number of

An excellent idea for recycling old nylons—the muted colors and original texture of this rug are obtained by braiding together old or discarded nylons. Designed by Hilary Dukes.

Chris Lewis

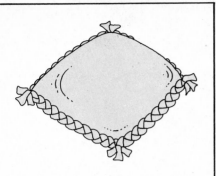

Use braids to trim a pillow.

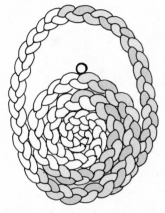

Make a handbag with two mats.

Join two lengths to make a belt.

Revamp last year's clothes with beautiful, bold braids.

different fabric colors and patterns available. For example, if you have a lot of a particular shade, with just a few scraps of other colors, make a feature of them. Alternatively, scatter them at random throughout the entire piece of work. Or if you have equal amounts of various colors, give strength to each by braiding a couple of coils in each color. Again, if there is more of one color than another,

either work a whole band from the smaller amount, or split it up into sections and stagger them to form a definite design. With a variety of different fabrics and colours you can create a handsome and unique article.

Basic working method

Preparing the strips. Cut or tear fabrics of similar thickness into strips, as long as possible. The width depends on the thickness of the material and what you are making. For rugs, work with 5cm-7.5cm (2″-3″) wide strips; for table mats, about 2.5cm-5cm (1″-2″). If they are cut too narrow it is difficult to turn under the edges neatly.

Fold the strips so that the raw edges meet in the middle of the wrong side of the fabric, then bring the folded edges together to make a flat strip with all raw edges enclosed (fig.1). You can

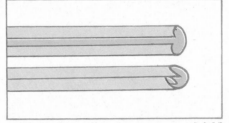

1. Fold edges of strip to center and fold strip in half, enclosing edges.

do this as you braid, but beginners are advised to press the fabric into its proper folds before braiding together. Keep the strips folded either by pinning, or by winding them around pieces of cardboard.

Braiding. To begin a 3-strand braid, unfold the raw edges of 2 strips and sew the ends together with a bias seam. Trim off corner (fig.2). Refold

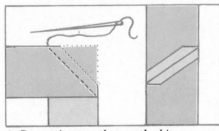

2. Sew strips together on the bias.

with the raw edges of the bias seam hidden inside. Attach the 3rd folded strip with a few stitches, to form a T (fig.3).

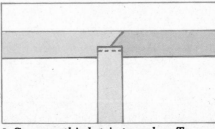

3. Sew on a third strip to make a T.

It is best to work with all the strips held taut. Secure the T end to a hook or door handle so that both hands are free for braiding.

Start by bringing the left-hand strip over the center strip and then the right-hand strip over that (fig.4). Continue

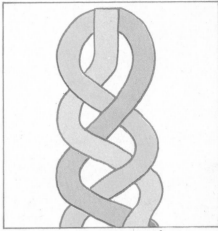

4. Braid the three strips together.

braiding, making sure that the folded edges are always toward the center of the braid. Keep the tension even, neither too tight nor too loose, and push the work up against the already braided end.

As you finish a strip, join on a new one with a bias seam.

If the lengths to be braided are very long, keep them wound around a piece of cardboard to prevent them from tangling and twisting. Make a slit in the edge of the cardboard to hold the working end; small amounts can then be released as required.

It is an advantage if the strips are uneven in length, so the joins will not be all in one place. Try to braid over a join so that it is hidden in the finished work. When introducing a new color, secure the completed braid with a safety pin to prevent it from unraveling, then turn in the ends of both new and old braids and sew them together edge to edge (fig.5). Make sure you keep the butted ends flat when sewing together.

5. Sew butted ends of braided strips.

Pauline Rosenthal

Make a charming and colorful set of table mats from scraps of toning fabrics. You can use any pieces of material that you have around the house that go well together. Choose complementary designs and colors.

Making up. As soon as you have braided about 60cm-90cm (2'-3'), begin sewing together. Lacing is the easiest and strongest method of connecting braids. Thread a blunt tapestry needle or bodkin (flat needle used for threading elastic) with either carpet thread or strong waxed cotton. Draw it through the loop of one braid, then thread through the corresponding loop of the braid opposite (fig.6).

When making a circular rug, wind the braid around and around, keeping it flat. This requires a little practice; if wound too tightly it will buckle, but it must not be too loose or the work will look rough and untidy. Ease in the fullness on the curves to keep the work flat.

When lacing together, it may be necessary to pass the needle through one loop on the inner braid and through two on the outer one.

To make an oval rug, begin with a long braid folded in half and laced together to give a long, shaped center. Wind around it, easing in the fullness where necessary.

Finishing. As you approach the end of the rug, start to taper the strips (fig.7). This will diminish the size of the braid so that it will gradually blend into the last braided row of the rug. Weave the remaining ends of the braid into the outer ring of the work—you may find a crochet hook helpful here. Slipstitch the ends invisibly to secure in place.

Backing. You may wish to line, or back the finished work. Choose a non-slip fabric if backing a rug or table mat. Place the finished article flat on the lining and cut to shape, allowing 1.5cm-2cm ($\frac{1}{2}''$-$\frac{3}{4}''$) all round for turnings. Turn in the edges of the lining and slipstitch to the back of the work.

Round nylon rug

Most women go through many pairs of stockings or panty hose every year. Instead of throwing them away once they are ruined, keep them—and ask all your friends to do so as well—then make them up into a tough, smart rug for the kitchen or bathroom. Panty hose are better to use than stockings as they are longer and therefore need fewer joins. Discard any that are very badly damaged as the runs will show in the finished rug.

To make a rug 90cm (3') in diameter:

You will need:

About 150 prs of panty hose or stockings

Nylon sewing thread

Sewing needle and bodkin

☐ Cut off and discard feet and reinforced tops.

☐ If the nylons are all of a similar color, bleach some of the legs in a weak solution of ordinary household bleach or commercial nylon bleach. Dye others dark brown.

☐ Sew the legs into strips, then braid them, taking care to mix the various shades effectively. Try to work 2 or 3 rounds that are predominantly pale and to finish with 2 or 3 rounds that are predominantly dark.

☐ Finish the rug in the usual way.

Round table mats

Worn or out-of-date cotton clothes are ideal for making table mats.

To make a set of 4 mats 40cm (16") in diameter:

You will need:

A total of 3m (3yd) of cotton fabric 90cm (36") wide—a set of 4 mats as shown uses about 1m (1yd) each of red, pink and orange sprigged cotton

Cotton thread

Sewing needle and bodkin

☐ Cut each color fabric into strips 2.5cm (1") wide and fold.

☐ Divide the colors equally into 4 mixed piles.

☐ Working with one pile, start by braiding 2 strands of one color to emphasize it, then mix all the colors, then make another color predominate. This will create strong, interesting

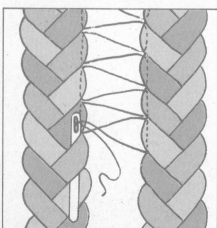

6. Lace coils together with a bodkin.

7. Weave away ends into last coil.

This attractive, cozy rag rug is made
*from long tweedy strips, braided together
in subtle combinations and coiled into
an oval.*

bands of color in the completed mat.
☐Finish in the usual way.
☐Make up the other 3 mats in the
same way, but do not attempt to make
the varying bands of color identical
in each mat. Part of their charm is that
each has its own unique qualities.

Oval tweed rug

A warm oval rug of this type would
look good in front of the fire, by the

bed or inside the front door.
You may be able to get hold of some
bags of scraps from a garment manu-
facturer—otherwise it's worth looking
through shapeless, unloved tweed and
woolen clothes at second-hand sales
for rock-bottom bargains.
To make this oval, multi-colored rug
90cm x 60cm (3′ x 2′):
You will need:
Tweed and woolen scraps adding up
to about 7m (8yd) x 90cm (36″).
Thread, sewing needle and bodkin
☐Cut fabric into strips 7.5cm (3″) wide.
☐Turn under the edges and fold.
☐Join and braid the strips. If the

colors are predominantly muted, with
only the occasional bright touch, try
to space out the bright pieces. Otherwise, work all the colorful pieces
together to make a band a little way
in from the edge.
☐Make the first braided length 30cm
(12″) long, before coiling and sewing
it up into an oval.

Pattern variations
You can go on to develop intricate rug
patterns on the lines of decorative
rush matting. For example, work an
oval center, surround it with round
panels sewn on firmly, then sew 2 or 3
rows of braiding all around the outside.

Sew a simple seating system

Cloth – sewing 1

Comfortable seating can be an expensive item of furnishing, but an encouraging aspect of modern seating is the way in which shapes have been getting simpler, less formally tailored, softer and more rounded—altogether easier to translate into do-it-yourself designs. Here is one of the easiest and most successful ideas—a bolster back cushion which props against the wall, on top of a plump base cushion.

It's specially designed to cut down the number of seams to a minimum.

The dimensions of this type of seating are the key to determining looks and comfort. Make sure that the base cushion is longer from front to back than it is wide or it will look stubby when the bolster is in place. And check that the height of the bolster doesn't exceed that of the base cushion or the chair will look top heavy.

Suitable cover fabrics. Virtually any fabric recommended for upholstery and slip covers will do, but avoid very thick, heavy cloths which are difficult to work with and cause build up at the corners. Also avoid velvet or any fabric with a pile which is likely to get crushed when in constant use. Even synthetic, furry fabrics tend eventually to lose their texture.

An all-wool, reversible fabric with a woven stripe has several advantages. Being reversible, it gives you a chance to enjoy a seasonal change of color schemes—like blue for winter and green for summer—and because it is woven in stripes (not printed) it makes cutting a straight seam extremely easy, an important consideration when making large cushions.

Any leftover strips of fabric can be used to make an attractive border for drapes.

The inner cushions consist of non-removable muslin covers filled with a mixture of crumbled foam and polystyrene pellets. Cut out and make muslin covers following the instructions given below for detachable covers, but cut them about 2.5cm (1") larger all around. The professional way to keep cushions looking trim and well filled is to make inner cushions slightly larger than the finished covers.

When stitching the muslin covers, use flat fell seams (see sewing know-how) and leave an opening in each, large enough to insert the filling.

Filling the cushions. A good mixture is 50% crumbled foam and 50% polystyrene pellets. When used on their own, crumbled foam mats into nasty chunks and polystyrene pellets are hard and uncomfortable—but a mixture of both makes a good texture. The polystyrene pellets constantly work through the foam to prevent it matting, so you need only mix them roughly when filling. When feeding in the crumbled foam, leave it in the plastic bag until right inside the muslin cover, to prevent it from spilling. Polystyrene pellets can be hard to manipulate until you know how. Quite simply, you need someone to hold the cover open while you pour in the pellets —either from a cardboard box with a hole cut out of one corner, or through a large funnel.

To fill one bolster and one base seat cushion you will need a total of 2.25kg (5lb) of crumbled foam and 2.25kg (5lb) of polystyrene pellets. When the cushions are full, sew up the openings firmly using thick cotton thread.

One of the easiest and most successful types of cushion seating to make yourself —a bolster back cushion which props against the wall on top of a square base cushion. This design cuts seaming to a minimum.

Basic sewing know-how

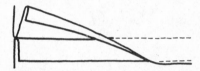

Flat fell seam: stitch seam in normal way and trim one seam allowance to 7mm ($\frac{1}{4}$"). Press seam to one side with wider allowance on top. Turn under edge of upper seam so it is even with trimmed seam. Pin in place and stitch close to folded edge.

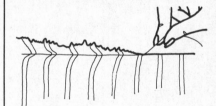

Finding the straight of grain by pulling a crosswise thread.

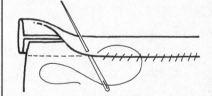

Attaching bias binding or tape.

Attaching snap fastener tape.

The cushion covers

Key to pattern pieces

A = base seat wrap-around

B = base seat end piece

C = bolster end piece

D = bolster wrap-around

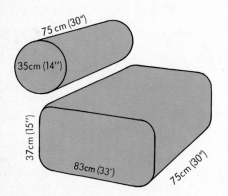

Large size seating

To make a seat 83cm x 75cm x 37cm (33″ x 30″ x 15″) and a bolster 75cm x 35cm (30″ x 14″).

You will need:
Length of fabric as given for layout 1 or 2
Matching thread
Snap fastener tape, 1.75m (5′9″) long
Bias binding or tape 2.5cm (1″) wide and 7.3m (8yd) long

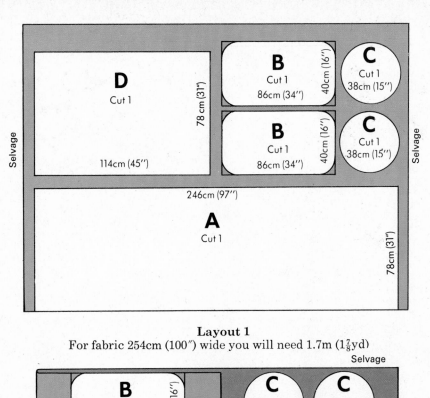

Layout 1
For fabric 254cm (100″) wide you will need 1.7m ($1\frac{7}{8}$yd)

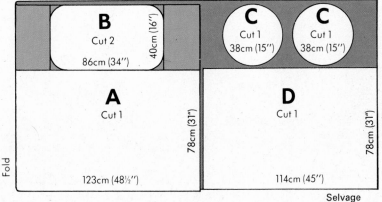

Layout 2
For fabric 119cm (47″) wide you will need 3.7m (4yd)

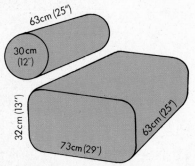

Smaller size seating

To make a seat 73cm x 63cm x 32cm (29″ x 25″ x 13″) and a bolster 63cm x 30cm (25″x 12″)

You will need:
Length of fabric as given for Layout 3
Matching thread
Snap fastener tape, 1.5m (5′) long
Bias binding or tape 2.5cm (1″) wide and 6.5m (7yd) long

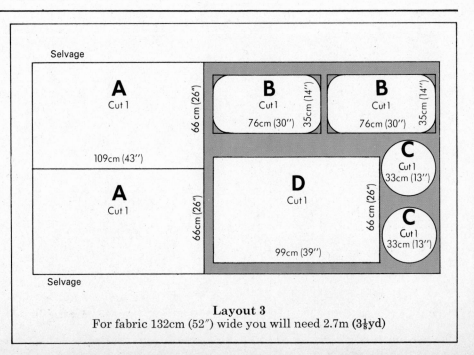

Layout 3
For fabric 132cm (52″) wide you will need 2.7m ($3\frac{1}{8}$yd)

16

Finishing

Depending on your fabric width, follow the relevant cutting layout. These allow for 1.5cm (½″) seams.

If you use a woven, striped fabric, make sure the stripes lie straight. Otherwise, make sure your selvages are straight. It is important to follow the layouts so that the pattern on the bolster and the seat run the same way and so that both side panels of the seat are identical.

The seat cushion and bolster can each be made out of a single, wrap-around piece of cloth, with two end pieces. Note: the smaller cushion (using 132cm (52″) fabric) needs one extra seam in place of fold line X shown in fig. 1. The end pieces are rectangular with

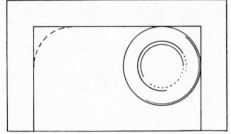

2. Use a dessert plate for corners.

rounded corners for the seat cushion, and circular for the bolsters. To cut the rounded corners, use a dessert plate to give a curve (fig.2).

For a reminder of basic sewing techniques, see previous page.

Finishing the seat cushion cover

☐Assemble pieces A and B as in fig.1, with right sides facing, and pin.

☐Stitch together with 1.5cm (½″) seams. Leave sides open where indicated by dotted lines in fig.1 and overcast or zigzag stitch the raw edges where snap fastener tape will be attached.

☐If the fabric is reversible bind the edges with contrasting bias binding or tape to give a piped effect to one side of the cushion covers and a flat finish to the other. If the fabric is not reversible, use plain bias binding or tape.

☐Turn under 1.5cm (½″) on the openings and attach the tape of snaps along the dotted lines (fig.1).

To make the bolster cushion cover

☐Cut a paper pattern for the end pieces by drawing a circle with a radius of 19cm (7½″) or 16.5cm (6½″) for smaller version, and cut (see layouts).

☐Prepare the edges of the bolster ends by making a row of small running stitches all around them and ease into the bolster. Pin and baste before you stitch, easing in the same way you would a sleeve into an armhole.

☐Stitch bolster, leaving a 46cm (18″) opening for snap fastener tape (fig.1).

☐Bind seams as for cushion.

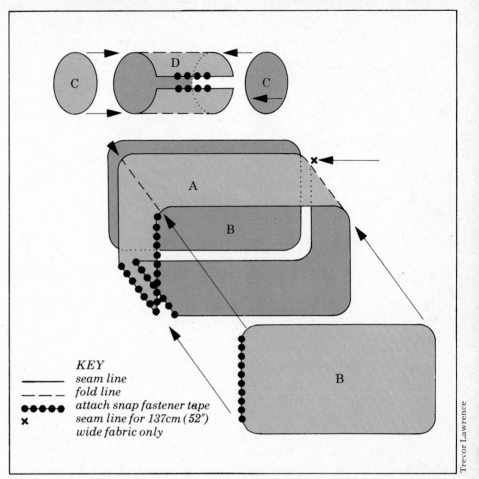

KEY
———	seam line
– – –	fold line
●●●●●	attach snap fastener tape
✕	seam line for 137cm (52″) wide fabric only

1. Assembly detail showing seam lines and where to sew the snap fastener tape.

Trevor Lawrence

Reversible covers enable you to enjoy a seasonal change of color scheme.

Starting with softwood

Carpentry is as easy to learn as cooking or dressmaking. It's surprising how quickly the few basic techniques can be mastered, and how satisfying and economical it is to build even the simplest of objects. It's really a matter of organizing the tools and materials, then following the directions step by step, carefully and patiently.

Jargon words like rabbet plane, spoke shave or ripsaw make woodwork sound much more difficult than it really is. These chapters set out to avoid the inhibiting language and introduce useful techniques clearly and simply.

The trivet in this chapter involves sawing, cutting and sanding. The only tools you need are a saw, a carpenter's square, steel tape and a chisel.

Softwoods and hardwoods

Wood is made up of long tubular cells like a bundle of drinking straws glued together. This structure makes wood much stronger in one direction than the other and it's much easier to cut along the cells or grain (ie to rip) than it is to cut across them (ie to cross-cut).

All pine or cone-bearing trees with needle pointed leaves, usually ever-greens, are softwoods, while all broad-leaved trees are classed as hardwood. Softwoods include pine, fir, redwood, spruce and many others. Hardwoods, include mahogany, teak, oak, birch and, surprisingly, balsa-wood. For most projects softwoods are best—being cheaper and easier to work with.

Selecting standard sizes

Most building supply stores or lumber yards hold a large selection of stock sizes. These are usually referred to by their sectional sizes: ie the thickness by the width. For example, you would ask for a 50mm x 100mm (2″x 4″) piece of pine, 2m (6′6″) long. In these chapters, the millimeters always refer to the sectional size and the centimeters or meters to the length.

The standard sizes refer to sawn wood so when buying prepared (ie planed) wood, the actual size will be fractionally smaller. The size of prepared wood can vary slightly from batch to batch, so always buy enough to complete a project. Select clean, straight pieces and try to look through the stock for those without knots, splits, or discoloration. For most projects any of the softwoods will do.

Tools

There is a great variety of special-purpose tools available. Many of these are for convenience only and most work can be done perfectly well using a minimum number of hand tools. Power tools are quicker to use, but unnecessary for basic projects.

Cutting tools must have a keen edge and are therefore potentially danger-ous. Never work on an uneven or unsteady surface: if you do not have a work bench, use a bench hook on the kitchen table.

Saw. There are many sizes and types of hand-saw. Almost any saw will do, but a small, light panel saw or a keyhole saw with interchangeable blades are both easy to handle and suitable for all small projects.

Carpenter's square. This is used to make guide lines for sawing and chisel-ling etc. Since it forms a rigid 90° angle its primary purpose is to make lines perpendicular to the edge of the lumber for cross-cutting. Use a sharp pencil to mark the line and if you have

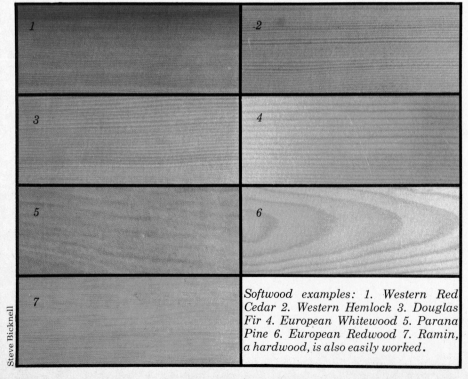

Softwood examples: 1. Western Red Cedar 2. Western Hemlock 3. Douglas Fir 4. European Whitewood 5. Parana Pine 6. European Redwood 7. Ramin, a hardwood, is also easily worked.

Steve Bicknell

Jerry Tubby

All these articles are made from soft-woods and illustrate some of the techniques used in woodwork. For example, the egg rack involves sawing with a coping saw and drilling; the candlestick is turned on a lathe; the salad servers are whittled. The wood can be finished in a number of ways, such as waxing, oiling and by the application of polyurethane.

a utility knife you can use it to score the wood; it severs the fibers and gives a cleaner cut.

Steel tape. A 3m (10′) retractable tape is recommended.

Chisel. A 6mm (¼″) is best for making this trivet.

You cannot do without the saw, but at a pinch you could do without the carpenter's square and use a ruler for measuring instead of a steel rule. You can use a screwdriver instead of the chisel, but you may ruin a good screwdriver and you will make a neater cut with a chisel.

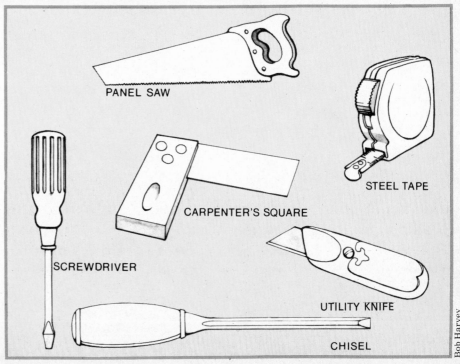

PANEL SAW

STEEL TAPE

CARPENTER'S SQUARE

SCREWDRIVER

UTILITY KNIFE

CHISEL

Bob Harvey

19

To make a bench hook

Spread an even layer of wood glue on the face of one strip. Lay this in position and rub to and fro across the particleboard. As air is squeezed from the joint, the glue forms a strong bond. Repeat for the second side and leave overnight to dry.

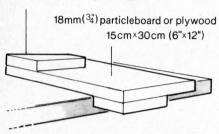

2 stop strips 25mm x 50mm (1"x 2") of softwood 100mm (4") long

18mm(¾") particleboard or plywood 15cm×30cm (6"×12")

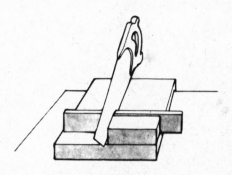

To make the trivet

This easy-to-make trivet can be used to protect the table or sideboard from hot casseroles or teapots.
For a trivet 19cm x 19cm (8"x 8"):
You will need:
A piece of softwood 12.5mm x 25mm (½"x 1"), 2m (6'6") long (allowing for some spare pieces)
Fine sandpaper
Optional—9 juniper disks from hobby shops, or slices of hardwood dowel, 3cm (1½") diameter; ask a wood dealer to cut them about 5mm (¼") thick
Wood glue
Tools: saw, steel tape, carpenter's square, chisel and utility knife.

---

1. To 'square off' the wood mark a line about 25mm (1") from the end with the carpenter's square. Place saw on edge of wood and draw it toward you to start the cut. Continue sawing, holding the saw vertically and using even, relaxed strokes.

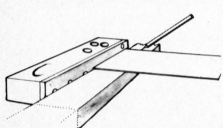

2. Measure off 19cm (8") from the squared off end and mark a line across. Make sure to saw on the outside of this line so the piece will be the full 19cm (8") long—the saw cut is about 2mm (1/10") wide.

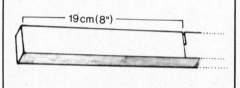

19cm(8")

3. Cut 7 pieces each 19cm (8") long (allowing one spare). On one piece:-
a) Mark off lengths shown along one 12.5mm (½") edge (using the square).
b) Align one of the other pieces along each of these lines and mark along the other side.

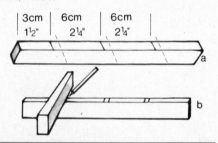

| 3cm 1½" | 6cm 2¼" | 6cm 2¼" |

---

4. Holding all the pieces together with ends even, use the square to continue the lines across the other 6 pieces.

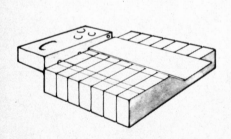

5. Mark 12.5mm (½") down both sides of each piece using a utility knife. This prepares for a clean cut at stage 6.

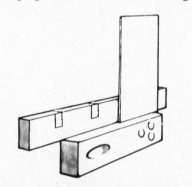

6. On all pieces make 6 cuts on the waste side or inside of each line, so the notch will be the exact width for the cross piece to fit tightly. (Cutting on the line would make notch about 2mm (1/10") too big.) First draw in the base lines of notches.

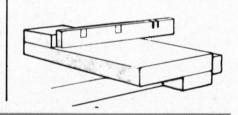

---

7. Put edge of chisel on base line, with sloping face on waste side, and push down. The waste will break off along the grain so, to avoid going over the marked line, work in stages. You might have to turn the wood over to get a square cut.

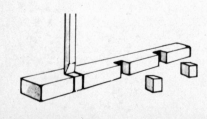

☐ Wrap the sandpaper around a block of wood and sand each piece. Finish by applying either furniture polish or clear, matt polyurethane.

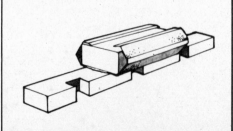

9. Slot the sections together.
10. Glue dowel disks (or juniper) as an alternative finish.

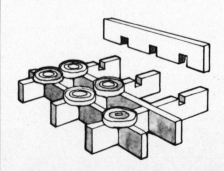

Alasdair Ogilvie

The number of cross sections can be increased to adapt the basic principle to other larger projects.

Other projects using this technique

Using this simple carpentry technique you can make a variety of interesting and useful projects. It is just a matter of a little practice to acquire confidence. Each time the technique is repeated it will be that much easier and faster.

The most important thing to remember when planning a project is to sit down with pencil and paper and draw the object and each piece individually. Indicate dimensions and make notes on how much lumber and which tools are necessary. Think out the project step by step, just as you followed each step for the trivet. This may take a little time but it's well worth it for, when it comes to the actual cutting, most of the planning will have already been worked out.

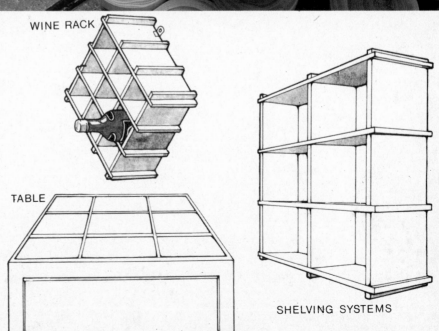

WINE RACK

TABLE

SHELVING SYSTEMS

How to make a mural with arcs

Color — paint 1

The first steps in using wall paints creatively are surprisingly easy and very effective. And on top of that, murals are great fun to paint. With non-drip paints it's easy to get a good finish, and with various cunning schemes you can achieve sophisticated and assured designs which don't require any freehand drawing ability. Look carefully at this mural and you will see that it is entirely built up of arcs, circles and straight lines. If the colors are not to your liking then imagine, for example, how cool it would look in shades of beige, cream and white (fig.2). And the arcs and circles system can be applied to all sorts of design ideas, some of which are developed below.

Basic drawing techniques

Arcs. To draw an arc larger than an ordinary compass can produce, tie a long piece of string to a pencil (fig.1); make a groove as close as possible to the sharpened end – this will prevent the string from slipping. Stab a thumb tack through the string to give the radius required. If you're right handed, use your left thumb to hold the drawing pin where you want the center of the circle, and draw your arc or circle. For very large arcs, ask a friend to hold the thumb tack while you draw the arcs.

Small circles. Small motifs, like flowers, can be made by clustering 4 or 5 circles drawn around drinking glasses and cups. For larger motifs, use various sizes of plates or dishes, even flower pots.

Ellipses. Draw shapes like rabbits' ears and leaves with 2 arcs, each drawn around a plate (fig.3).

Ovals. Use a dinner plate to draw 2 circles just touching each other. With a ruler, draw 2 lines at a tangent to the tops and bottoms of the circles. This is a simple system for drawing shapes like sheep's bodies. Add a head drawn from a small plate, stick legs, and a scalloped line around the body for a wooly effect (fig.4).

Composite shapes. To make shapes like clouds and foliage, take a sheet of newspaper, brown wrapping paper or cardboard and use dinner plates to construct intersecting arcs to make up an irregular mass. When it looks satisfactory, cut all around the outside and use this as a template to draw the shape on the mural (fig.5). To use the template but vary the effect, turn it over and reverse the pattern.

To prepare the wall. Wipe down and apply an undercoat of white emulsion (water-based paint). If the area you want to paint is square, divide the side and ceiling edges into 4 equal sections. Ask a friend to stand on a chair and hold a long piece of string weighted with a heavy object from each marked point. Lightly pencil in the lines from ceiling to floor. Mark off these vertical lines into 4 equal sections and draw a line across with a straight edge. If the wall is wider than it is high, start from the extreme left or right, mark off a square based on floor to ceiling height, and divide as before. Extend the grid to fill the rest of the wall.

Suitable paints. Quick-drying paint like emulsion is best, preferably the non-drip variety.

To make the Springtime mural

The mural shown is painted on a wall 2.4m (8′) square. The design works on any square area; simply adjust the scale as required.

You will need:
White emulsion for undercoat
One liter (1qt) sky blue emulsion; small amounts of mauve, candy pink, orange, yellow, light green, mid-green
Brushes in various sizes

☐ Prepare wall.

☐ Mark off into 16 squares and label as shown. Extend grid for oblong wall.

☐ Right hill: with center 1D and radius 1D-1B, draw arc from 1B to line E. Left hill: with center 1A and radius 1A-3A, make arc from 3A to meet right hill. Center hill: with center 1C and radius 1C-3C, draw arc to intersect left and right hills.

☐ Rainbow: with center at intersection

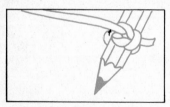

1. Attach string to pencil.

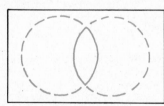

3. Drawing rabbit's ears.

4. Draw sheep using 2 plates.

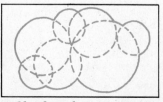

5. Clouds and trees composite.

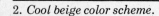

2. Cool beige color scheme.

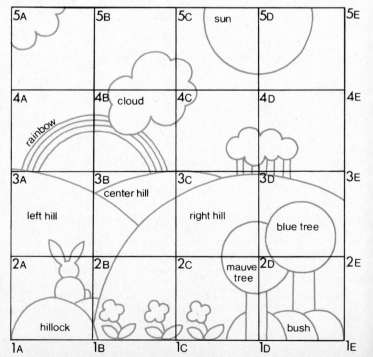

Victoria Drew

22

Springtime mural in sunshine colors to liven up dull or plain walls, designed by Juliet Glynn-Smith.

Left: square off the wall and draw in the shapes for the mural. For an oblong wall extend the hills and the cloud or repeat with a mirror image.

of left and center hill, and radius $\frac{2}{3}$ of distance from thumb tack to 3A, draw arc. With same center make 3 more arcs about 8cm (3″) apart.

☐Blue tree: to find the center of the blue tree; with center 2D and radius just over $\frac{1}{2}$ of 2D-2E, draw an arc. Repeat with center 2E, and intersect first arc. This intersection is the center point of the blue tree. With this center and radius just short of line E, draw a complete circle.

☐Mauve tree: with center 2D and same radius as blue tree, draw an arc. For trunks, make bands with straight edge.

☐Bushes: with center 1D and radius $\frac{1}{3}$ 1D-1C, draw an arc to intersect bottom line. With center where right

hand point of first bush meets line 1, and same radius, make another arc. Repeat to make 3rd bush.

☐Hillocks: with center at mid 1A-1B, and radius $\frac{1}{2}$ 1A-1B, draw a semicircle. With center 1B and same radius, draw small arc.

☐Sun: with center on line D, 8cm (3″) down from 5D, and radius $\frac{3}{4}$ 5D-4D, draw an arc.

☐Trees on horizon: on a piece of cardboard make a composite shape with teacups. Move template around until it is in a satisfactory position, draw around it and mark in the trunks.

☐Rabbit: use 25cm (10″) dinner plate for body, 18cm (7″) small plate for head, average teacup for tail and large coin for nose. Make ellipses with small plate for ears.

☐Flower: make a cardboard template, using teacup for petals and small plate for leaves and stem.

☐Clouds: use dinner plate to make a composite shape.

Start painting by first outlining

areas of different color and filling in large areas. Example: outline the clouds and sun in blue and then paint the sky. Work from top to bottom in this way so any drips from the top can be covered.

To get a clean edge on curves, keep plenty of paint on the brush and use the side, drawing it along gently, rather than using the tip. Keep brushes clean to avoid muddying the colors. Let first coat dry thoroughly before applying 2nd. Yellow may need 3 coats.

Alternative design ideas

Develop the rainbow theme to cover a wall entirely with arcs, and paint in graduated tones of pale colors. Overlap arcs to build up a complete fishscale pattern, then paint blue and silver for a bathroom. Use dinner plate clusters for huge red poppies, or separate plates for a cloud, balloons or bubbles in a bathroom. Or paint a friendly flock of white sheep on a pale blue nursery wall.

Begin with wire jewelry

Because most people tend to think that working with metal involves using heavy machinery, it is rather neglected as a craft material. But primitive man did marvelous things with the minimum of tools and now modern, small-scale aids make it possible for anyone to take up a wide variety of metal-working techniques at home. And since metal is so versatile the creative design possibilities are endless, once the basic techniques are mastered.

These chapters are arranged in a progressive order of techniques, so you can acquire tools gradually.

Wire

Many early pieces of jewelry were based on patterns created with wire which had been made by hand. As an introduction to the possibilities of working with metal, interesting jewelry can be made from various types of wire. The techniques can be developed to form very intricate pieces and wire combines well with other materials, like leather and all kinds of stones. Economically, it is a good idea to start with copper, brass or silver-plated wire. Once you acquire the knack of bending the wire in various ways you can graduate to fine silver wire.

Care. Keep stocks of wire labeled with their thickness or gauge number until you have learned to recognize the various sizes. Wrap the wire up in plastic bags to prevent discoloration when you are not working with it. Always keep wire as straight as possible. If the wire has been kept in a large coil it can be straightened by lightly smoothing it with the fingers.

Polish and finishing. Clean the completed pieces by immersing them in a liquid silver cleaner. Wash in soapy luke-warm water and dry. To prevent future discoloration, spray with a metal or clear varnish. If the silver is being used with other materials, clean it thoroughly first.

Joins. Note how joined pieces hang. The pieces do not stay flat but alternate – one flat and the other at right angles to it (fig.1). Designs must follow this pattern otherwise the piece of jewelry will not hang in the correct way. A piece of work will never appear the

1

same when lying on the work bench as when it is suspended, so always hold your work up to look at it.

It is difficult to correct or straighten a piece of wire without it looking untidy and overworked so, if a mistake is made, it is better to start again with a new piece of wire.

You can use the discarded pieces for making jump rings.

Tools

Round-nosed pliers do not have to be expensive but check that the jaws make contact along their entire length. The inside of the jaw should be smooth otherwise it will damage the surface of the wire. If they are not smooth, cover the jaws with a bandaid, although this does make it slightly more difficult to grip heavy wire firmly. All-in-one pliers that cut and bend round and square lines are only suitable in the early stages. Once more

This intricate sunray necklace is not nearly as difficult to make as it looks.

the front of the pliers and a large one with it at the back.

The end of the wire in the jaws should not stick out beyond the pliers. Grip the pliers firmly and turn in a clockwise direction using the thumb of the other hand to apply pressure to the wire close to the jaws. You can work in a counterclockwise direction if it is easier but whichever way you do, make it a habit to work in the same direction. Try to complete a curl without having to regrip the wire.

Diagonal wire cutters or end cutters. It is easier to cut jump rings with the diagonal wire cutters, but either these or end cutters will do.

Metal file. You can use a medium sized metal file or you can buy a selection of Swiss or needle files. You will not need all the files to make the pieces shown here, but it is economical to buy a set of about 6 as they will be useful later.

It is sensible to spend as much as you can afford on tools, all of which can be bought from a hardware store.

Bracelet with bead

You will need:
18cm (7″) of 1.5mm (15 gauge) silver-plated wire
One bead that will fit onto wire
☐File ends of wire and thread the bead. Shape with fingers and make a curl at each end to hook together.

Earrings

You will need:
31cm (12″) of 1.5mm (15 gauge) silver-plated wire
A pair of earring clasps, clip-on or screw type, available from craft shops, notions stores or jewelers. The clasps must have a hook or eye to which a jump ring can be attached.

Jump rings are used to attach and assemble jewelry. Make 2 jump rings by placing the end of the wire halfway down the jaws and working it around until you have 2 complete circles (fig.2).
☐Line up the end cutters with the end of the wire and cut through both coils (fig.3).

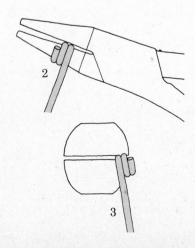

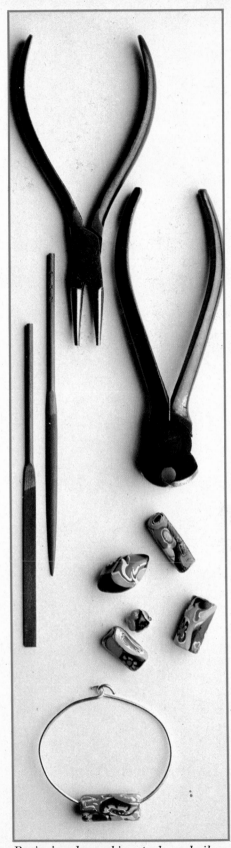

Basic jewelry-making tools and silver-plated wire bracelet with bead.

progressive techniques are reached a higher quality of tool is required.
Curling with round-nosed pliers. The size of the curl depends on the position of the wire in the jaws of the pliers. A small curl is made with the wire at

☐File ends of rings flat and smooth.
☐To make a larger number of jump rings coil the wire around any cylindrical shape of the right size (fig.4).

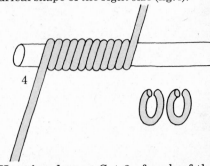

Hanging drops. Cut 2 of each of the lengths shown in fig.5 and file ends.

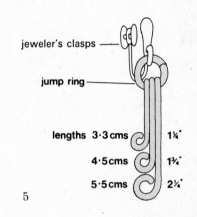

jeweler's clasps

jump ring

lengths	3·3 cms	1¼″
	4·5 cms	1¾″
	5·5 cms	2¼″

5

☐Make a small loop at one end of each piece of wire (fig. 6). These will thread onto the jump rings.

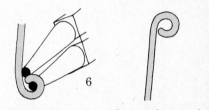

6

Victoria Drew

☐The curls at the other end must be made at right angles to the loop. You must curve 3 pieces in a clockwise direction and 3 in counterclockwise direction. To do this divide the lengths of wire into 2 equal groups so that you have the same number of equal lengths in each pile.

Working from one pile, hold the loop to curve away from yourself and make a curl at the other end so that it is in a vertical position when the loop is in a horizontal one.

Make a small curl for the short piece of wire and increase to larger curls for the other 2 pieces, the longest piece having the largest curl.
☐Repeat with the other 3 pieces but hold the loop so that it curves toward you. Assemble the pieces with the jump rings and findings as illustrated. Close the jump rings using the pliers. When doing this do not hold the earring in such a way as to bend any of the pieces.

The curvy bracelet

You will need:

38cm (15″) of 1.5mm (15 gauge) silver-plated wire

☐At the center of the wire make a large curl with the pliers to let the wire cross about 2.5cm (1″) from the curve. Bend as shown in fig. 7.

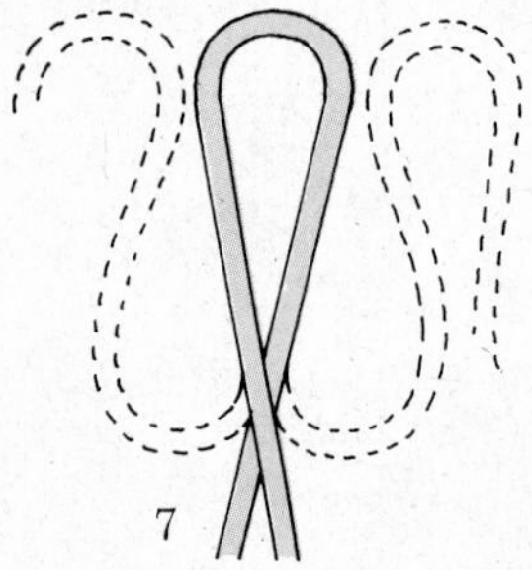

☐Make the next curve where the wire crosses and continue to form the pattern illustrated.

☐Bend the wire with your fingers so that it fits round the wrist. The bracelet is not circular but elliptical.

☐Bend each end into a U-shape so that they hook into one another.

The size of the bracelet can be varied by opening or closing the angles of the curves.

The pendant

You will need:

91cm (37″) of 1.5mm (15 gauge) silver-plated wire

45cm (18″) of 0.6mm (23 gauge) silver-plated wire for the thong

Leather thong 56cm (22″) long, about 5mm (¼″) in diameter

☐The 6 suspended pieces on the inside of the horseshoe (fig.8) are made in the same way as the 6 earring pieces.

☐Make the horseshoe with 16cm (7″) of wire. File the ends and fold the wire around a cylindrical object of 3cm (1¼″) diameter. Do this by holding the halfway point of the wire to the cylinder with one hand using the thumb to keep the wire firmly in position. With the other hand work the wire around the cylinder, starting by applying pressure to the wire closest to the thumb of the other hand. Bend the wire until the ends meet (fig.9).

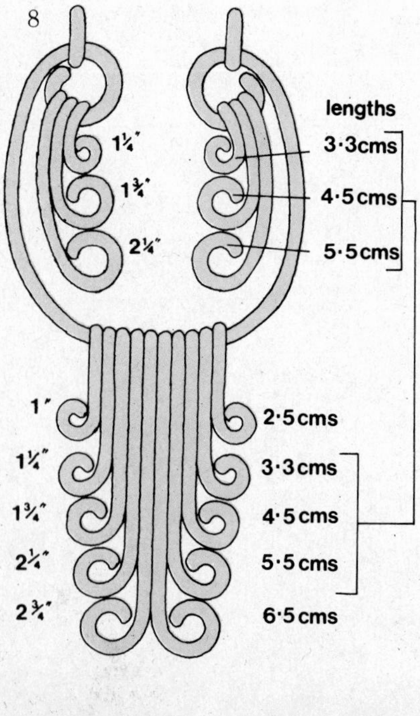
8
1¼″
1¾″
2¼″
lengths
3·3cms
4·5cms
5·5cms
1″
1¼″
1¾″
2¼″
2¾″
2·5cms
3·3cms
4·5cms
5·5cms
6·5cms

☐To make the 10 suspended pieces at the bottom of the horseshoe cut 2 each of the following lengths:

2.5cm (1″), 3.3cm (1¼″), 4.5cm (1¾″), 5.5cm (2¼″), 6.5cm (2¾″).

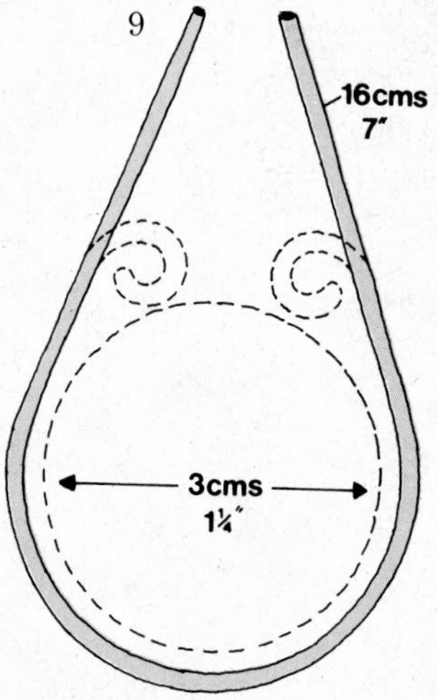
9
16cms
7″
3cms
1¼″

☐File the ends and make a small loop at one end of each piece. Divide the pieces into 2 groups and proceed as for the earrings. The 3 shorter pieces from one pile are made with small curls, the next piece is slightly larger and the longest piece has the largest curve.

☐Thread the pieces onto the horseshoe to form the pattern illustrated.

☐Make a large curl at each end of the horseshoe but do not close them completely. Thread the 6 pieces and close the open ends.

☐Make any adjustments to the pieces to even out the pattern.

☐Make 2 jump rings and hook them through the 2 curls on the horseshoe. Close the jump rings and thread the leather thong through them.

Hook and eye closure. For the thong use the 0.6mm (23 gauge) wire.

☐For the eye use 20cm (8″) of wire and make a loop 3cm (1½″) from the end of the wire (fig.10).

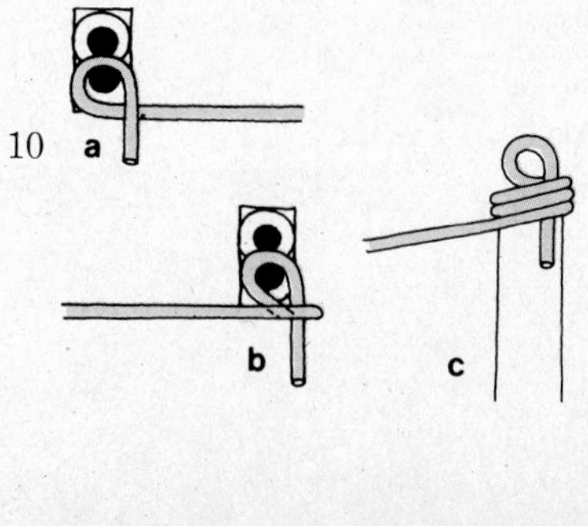
10
a
b
c

☐Wind the long end of the wire around the thong 4 times. You may find it easier to do this if you start a short distance from the end of the thong and trim it when you have finished.

☐Cut off the short end of the wire and continue winding the wire to the end. Press the end firmly into the thong with the pliers, without damaging the coils.

☐To make the hook use the remaining wire and make a U-shape 5cm (2″) from the end (fig.11). Start winding the wire around the thong 2.5cm (1″) from the end of the U-shape and proceed as before.

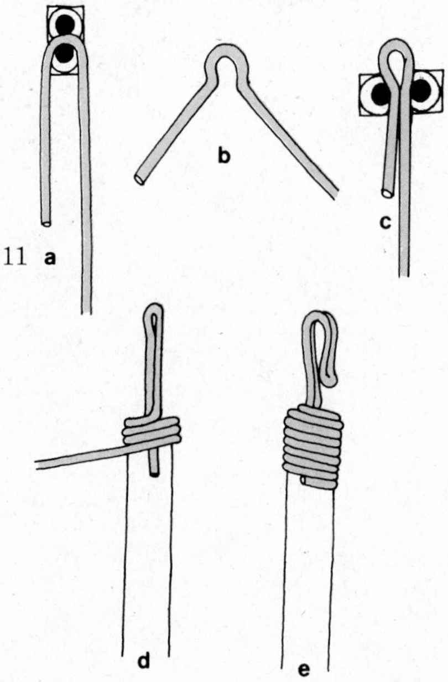
11
a
b
c
d
e

☐Bend the end around to form a hook and make any adjustment necessary so that it fits the eye.

Preparing designs

Once you have a working knowledge of different wires you can design your own jewelry. Always start by drawing a full-scale, linear diagram with a felt-tipped pen to the same thickness as the wire you intend to use. Make your motifs according to this diagram or a prototype made from it.

It is difficult to make every section identical, but by using the diagram you can retain the scale, which gives an overall unity to the design. The discrepancies between the various sections give the piece its original appearance, impossible to achieve when similar articles are mass produced.

The sunray necklace (page 24)

You will need:

3m (10′) of 1.5mm (15 gauge) silver-plated wire

The individual pieces must be made as near identical as possible otherwise they will not hang evenly when linked together. The pieces are joined together by 2 equal loops made at right angles to one another and interlinked.

☐ Cut a 6.5cm (2½″) piece of wire.

☐ Use this for measuring and cut another 43 pieces of the same length.

☐ File one end of each piece flat.

☐ Cut 8cm (3″) of wire and file one end. Make a large loop for the eye at the filed end by putting the wire right

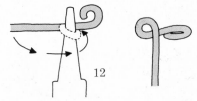

into the jaws of the pliers. Make the 2nd loop using the pliers about 5mm (¼″) from the front (fig.12). The loops for all the following pieces, except the last one, must be made in exactly the same position.

☐ Working from the pile and using the pliers in the same position throughout, make an open loop at the filed end to form a hook shape. Insert this through the 2nd loop of the previous piece and

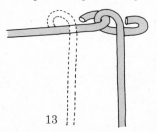

close the hook (fig.13).

☐ Hold the 2nd piece in the position used in fig.1 and curl the wire around to complete the pattern.

☐ Repeat for all the pieces of wire.

☐ To make the hook cut a 12cm (4½″) piece of wire and file one end. Make a hook and insert it through the 2nd curl of the previous piece and close the hook. Make a U-shape 2.5cm (1″) from this curl (fig.14). Fold the end over

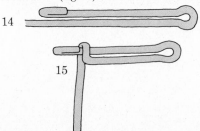

near the first curl and complete the pattern (fig.15). Fold the length of U-shape in half to complete the hook. Suspend the piece over an upturned mixing bowl. Make any adjustment necessary so the hook and eye fit.

☐ Trim the individual pieces so that they are all of the same length. File the ends and make any adjustment necessary to let the pieces hang at the same angle.

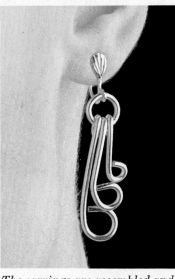

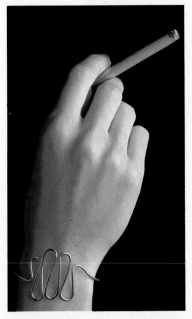

The earrings are assembled and attached to jump rings:

Steve Bicknell

A series of curls form the curvy bracelet, left. The pendant above develops into a large necklace, below left. Hang the completed necklace over an upturned mixing bowl and make adjustments to it so that it hangs evenly. If you make the sunray necklace, below right, from silver wire, first use cheaper wire to practice making the two pieces at the

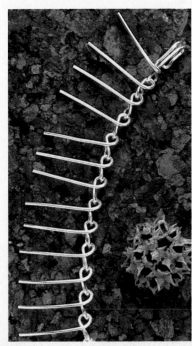

Circles, arcs and right angles

Right angles

Enlarging a design onto a surface, picture framing and woodwork often require an exact rectangle to be drawn, and many designs need to be assembled to an exact right angled (90°) shape.

You will need: Ordinary compass or pencil, string and thumb tack; ruler or steel tape.

☐Draw a horizontal line, which will be one side of the right angle. Mark off a point A, 3 units from the end – the bigger the units you can afford to use the better. Set the span of your compass or piece of string to 5 units, place the pin at A and draw an arc. Now set the span of your compass or string to 4 units and, with the pin at B, draw a second arc to intersect with the first at C (fig.4). The line BC will be at right angles with the line AB. A right angle is normally indicated by a small square, as in the diagram. This method depends on the fact that all triangles with sides in the ratio 3:4:5 have a right angle between the two shorter sides.

When carrying out design projects, you often need to be able to construct exact geometrical shapes. Here is a reminder of how to draw circles, arcs and right angles, the bases of many interesting designs.

Circles

The diameter of a circle is the distance across the circle measured at its widest point, and the radius is half the diameter.

You will need: A compass or pencil, string and thumb tack.

☐To draw circles with diameters up to 30cm (12″), use a compass. Set the arms so that they are the radius of the projected circle apart, place the pin arm firmly where the center of the circle is to be, and let the pencil arm swing freely around to make a perfect circle (fig.1).

☐Larger circles can be drawn just as simply using the string and thumb tack method. Cut a notch in a pencil, as close to the sharpened end as possible, and tie one end of a length of string to it. Push the thumb tack through the other end of the string to give exactly the radius of the circle. Keeping thumb firmly on the thumb tack pull the string taut and draw the circle (fig.2). To find the circumference (C) of a circle, use the formula $C = 2\pi R$. R is the radius, π (pronounced pie) is $^{22}/_7$. So, for a radius of 14cm, $C = 2 \times {}^{22}/_7 \times 14$cm $= 88$cm.

Arcs

Sections of circles, known as arcs, are also useful in planning murals or needlework designs. A variety of decorative effects can be achieved by combining arcs and circles to form a pleasing arrangement.

A fishscale pattern for patchwork, or border decorations in any material, can be made on the same principle.

Draw a horizontal line and, using a compass or the string and thumb tack method according to the size of the design, make a series of semicircles butting up against each other on the line. Draw a line across the top of the semicircles (fig.3) and mark point A half-way between points B and C. Keeping the same radius as before, place the pin at point A and draw a semicircle that passes through points B and C. Repeat all along the row to form the 2nd layer of fishscales, and construct all further layers in the same way to the required depth.

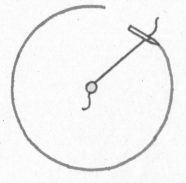

2. Larger circles can be drawn using string and pencil.

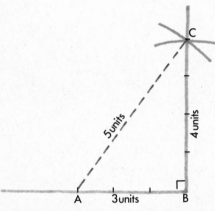

4. Making a right angle.

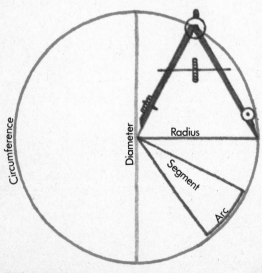

1. The circle.

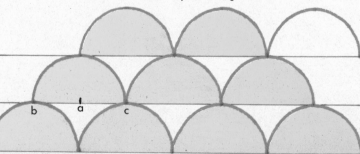

3. Repeated layers of semicircles can be used to make a fishscale pattern.

Victoria Drew

Creative ideas 1

Dough Sculpture

Sculpting with dough is fun. It's also inexpensive because all you need is flour, salt and water. You can make all shapes of baskets depending on what you choose for a mold. It is then baked so the mold must be ovenproof.

To make the basket shown:

You will need:

30cm (12″) round baking dish, 6.5cm (2½″) deep
Small pastry brush, or paint brush; wooden skewer or sharp pencil; clean damp cloth; aluminum foil; baking sheet; clear polyurethane varnish.

For the dough:

1½ average-size cups of salt
6 cups of flour
2¼ cups of hot water
1 egg for glazing the finished basket

☐ Cover the outside of the baking dish with foil, folding the excess inside the dish.

☐ In a medium size bowl add the water to the salt and stir occasionally until the salt is dissolved. Leave to cool.

☐ Slowly add to the flour, mixing with your hands as the dough will be very stiff.

☐ Knead the dough on a pastry board until it is smooth and pliable. If the dough becomes too wet, knead in more flour, if it is too stiff, add a few drops of water.

The dough soon dries and becomes brittle when exposed to air, so work quickly and keep any unused dough wrapped up in a damp cloth.

☐ Using ¾ of the dough, roll it on a lightly floured flat surface into a rectangle about 35cm x 45cm (14″x18″) and 3mm (⅛″) thick.

☐ The dough is then cut into strips 2cm (¾″) wide. For the baking dish recommended you will need 6 strips 43cm (17″) long, 4 strips 40cm (16″) long and 4 strips 29cm (12″) long. For a differ-

ent size dish, invert the dish and measure over the center from rim to rim to find the longest strips. Then cut the others proportionately. Keep the leftovers wrapped in a damp cloth.

☐ Place a piece of foil 45cm (18″) square on a table top and position half the strips

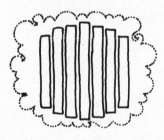

1

as in fig.1, leaving about 2cm (¾″) spaces between them. Begin to weave with one of the 43cm (17″) pieces through the center of those on the foil. Continue to weave the strips, working from the center out.

☐ To make the basket more secure glue all the intersections formed by the 43cm (17″) strips with a little

2

water brushed between the layers (fig.2). Press through the center of each intersection with the point of the skewer. Be careful not to stretch the strips as you weave, and if they break, mend them with a little water.

☐ Turn the baking dish upside down. Lift up the lattice work on the foil, holding the edge of the foil firmly. Center and slowly lower

3

over the dish (fig.3).

☐ Lift the dish, tuck the excess foil underneath and trim the strips even with the dish edge, using a very sharp knife. Mold the lattice to the dish by pressing lightly with your hands. Where the 40cm (16″) and 29cm (12″) strips intersect, glue with water and skewer as before. Place on a baking sheet, bottom up, and cover with a damp cloth.

☐ Knead the scraps and the reserved ¼ of dough until smooth. Using your palms, roll the dough on a flat surface into two ropes about 105cm (42″) long and 12mm (½″) thick. Place them side

by side and begin winding together one over the other to form a twist.

☐ Attach them to the basket edge by brushing the ends of the lattice strip with water and wrapping the twist around the edge, pressing it gently so that it sticks. Wet the overlapping ends of the twist to finish.

☐ In a moderate oven, bake the basket for 30 minutes.

☐ Prepare a glaze by mixing the egg with a teaspoon of water. Take the basket from the oven and remove the dish by pulling up the edges of foil. Return the basket to the baking sheet upside down and brush over with the egg mixture. Bake for 15 minutes. Repeat the glazing process every 15 minutes, alternating right side and wrong side up until it is a golden brown and thoroughly dry. Leave to cool on a wire rack.

☐ When everything is cool, apply several coats of clear varnish, allowing it to dry completely between coats.

Pop-up cards – fan folds

This chapter takes the pop-up principle shown in Paper, chapter 1 and demonstrates how it can be developed to create all sorts of interesting effects. The pop-up cards shown here are based on a triangle folded from the center crease of the card. The airplane trail is a simple pop-up triangle, the elephant and the peacock combine the triangular pop-up shape with a cut inner edge.

To make pop-up triangle

Fold the paper in half twice to make the card shape, then open up the card and re-fold it in the vertical crease (see Paper, chapter 1). Fold down one corner from half way down the central crease to half way along the upper edge (fig.1). Press sharply. Fold the crease over the other way and repeat once or twice to make the crease workable. Re-fold the card, and with the thumb and forefinger of the left hand keeping the crease in position, use the fingers of the right hand to ease the triangular pop-up shape into position (fig.2). Carefully ease the card closed, then work it open and shut once or twice so the pop-up operates freely.

The instructions for making the cards show how to create effects with colored gummed papers—but you may prefer just to draw the outlines, or to use crayons, paints or colored inks.

Once you have tried these ideas, you will be able to think of many others—the elephant can turn into a dog, the peacock's tail into a dress, the airplane trail into the rays of the Christmas star. It's not essential for the inside fold to be the same length as the outside one. The peacock's tail could just as well come half-way down the card, with the hedge stuck or painted to the inside back of the card. But it is important to get the balance right or the card may topple forward.

It's also advisable to work out new ideas on ordinary ruled paper before using more expensive, stiff paper

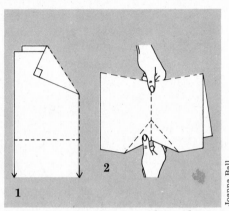

Joanna Ball

1,2. *Fold the pop-up triangle as shown.*

To make the airplane card

You will need:

Pale blue construction paper 20cm x 30cm (8″x12″)

White gummed paper 20cm x 10cm (8″x4″)

Scraps of green, red and white gummed paper

Scissors, coins or compass, ruler, glue

☐ Take the pale blue paper, fold in half twice to make 10cm (4″) by 15cm (6″), and make the triangular pop-up shape described above.

☐ Cut out the cloud shape from the white gummed paper, using various coins or a compass and a variety of radii to make arcs along one 20cm (8″) edge. Cut out the clouds.

☐ Fold cloud shape in half to find center line, and fold a triangle from center crease to the same dimensions as pop-up shape. Cut this triangle out of the cloud shape, and stick the cloud on exactly over pop-up.

☐ Trace the airplane and cut it out of the green gummed paper.

☐ Fold it in half to give the center line, and stick the airplane onto the card so that the center creases coincide. Use red and white gummed circles with inked center for roundels.

Chris Lewis

To make the peacock card

You will need:

Dark blue construction paper 20cm x 30cm (8″x12″)

20cm (8″) squares of green and white gummed paper

Scraps of dark blue and brown gummed paper

Small gold circular stickers

Scissors, compass, ruler, glue, small coin

☐ Fold the dark blue paper in half twice to make 10cm (4″) by 15cm (6″).

☐ Using the compass and a 10cm (4″) radius, draw an arc from the center corner on the lower edge to the outer edge of the card (fig.3). Mark the point where the pin of the compass was placed. Take the small coin and place it half-way over the center crease, against the arc. Move the coin along and draw a series of semicircles side by side along the edge of the arc (fig.4).

☐ With the card folded along the vertical crease, cut out the tail shape through both thicknesses of paper (fig.5).

☐ Make the triangular pop-up shape by folding sharply from the marked point to 2½ scallops from the center edge (see fig.6).

Re-fold the card and ease the pop-up into position.

☐ Cut a piece of green gummed paper 12cm x 20cm (5″x8″) wide and stick it to the inside back of the card to form the background to the tail.

☐ Trace the shape above the peacock's fan, cut it out of white gummed paper and stick it in position to form sky.

☐ Trace the peacock's body from the shape given here, cut out of dark blue paper and stick in position.

☐ Draw a line from the marked point where pin of compass was placed to the edge of the 2nd-to-last semicircle on each side. Then trace the areas

down to these lines and cut the hedge out of green paper, using the small coin again to give the scalloped edge. Stick in position.

☐ Decorate the peacock's tail with blue, brown and gold circles.

☐ Cut 2 semicircles of white paper for the eye, inking a black pupil in the lower half.

3,4,5,6. *Draw scalloped edge of peacock tail, cut out and fold as shown.*

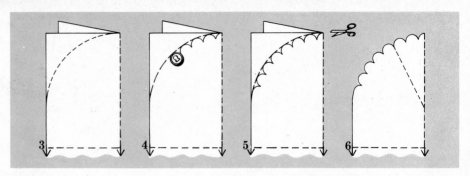

To make the elephant card
You will need:
Pale gray construction paper 20cm x 30cm (8″x12″)

Dark brown gummed paper 12cmx20cm (5″x8″)

Scraps of black, white gummed paper

Scrap of thick white paper

Scissors, compass, ruler, glue

☐ Fold the gray paper in half twice to make 10cm (4″) by 15cm (6″). Open up the card and re-fold it into the vertical crease.

☐ Draw or trace the elephant face shape given here and draw it on the edge of the card (fig.7). Cut out.

☐ Fold the card back between the center of the card and the point between the elephant's face and ear (fig.8). Work the crease to and fro a few times.

☐ Draw the circular body shape on the brown paper, using the compasses with a 5cm (2″) radius.

Draw the elephant's legs 2.5cm (1″) wide and 2.5cm (1″) apart. Cut the shape and stick the outline to the card.

☐ Cut out black and white circles from gummed paper for the eyes, with an inked dot in the center for the pupil.

☐ Cut 3 small circles from black paper, and cut each one in half to give 6 semi-circular toe-nails. Stick in position on the bottom of the legs.

☐ Trace the tusk from the shape given here and cut 2 from the thick white paper. Stick one on each side of the trunk, gluing them onto the underside of the face.

For a late card, an elephant that never forgets! Designed by Joanna Ball.

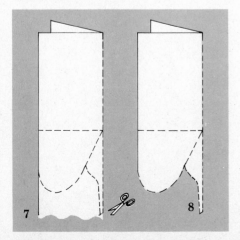

7,8. *Cut out elephant's face and fold.*

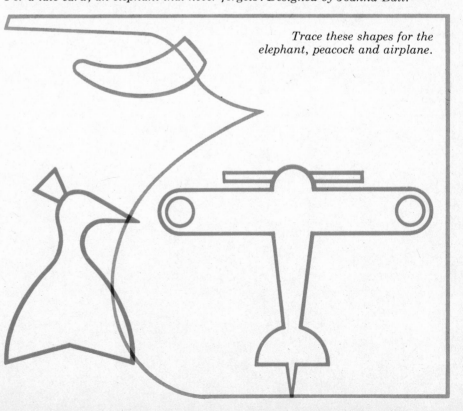

Trace these shapes for the elephant, peacock and airplane.

Clear cast embedding

Plastic is a lightweight material and is easily worked. It comes in liquid form as a polyester resin or it can be a solid such as acrylic plastic. Therefore you either pour or cut it accordingly. Plastic is at its best when transparent or translucent. Unlike glass, it does not simply let light pass through it but diffuses it and carries it along its length, even around curves in a rod, to give the edge a fluorescent light. You can make all sorts of beautiful, modern designs in plastic, such as chess pieces, paper weights, jewelry, door knobs, magazine racks and trays.

If you think of plastic only as a substitute for materials such as glass, wood or metal, then you should reconsider. Plastic comes in an exciting variety of forms and colors and behaves in a completely different way from any other material.

Plastic is made up of chemicals derived from coal and petroleum and this chemical structure can be altered to suit different purposes.

Plastic is really a collective word for a number of materials, many quite unlike one another. However, they can be divided into two main groups.

Thermoplastics

These are plastics which are hard at normal temperatures but soften when heated. The temperature needs to be controlled to prevent the plastic from bubbling and therefore shrinking. The material can be shaped and molded and will retain the new shape when it cools to its former solid mass. This process can be repeated a number of times before the material starts to break down. This means that if you make a mistake it can be corrected.

Acrylic in sheets or rods, celluloid, polystyrene and PVC are all examples of thermoplastics.

Thermosetting plastics

These are a group of materials that undergo a chemical change which is irreversible. They solidify in the presence of heat and, once shaped and cooled, they cannot be reworked. They can be reinforced with fiberglass which makes them strong enough to be used for structural purposes.

Polyester resins are thermosetting plastics. They have a syrup-like con-sistency and, when mixed with a catalyst—the hardener—they generate heat and then cool down to a solid. Resins are made for different applications so always make sure that the resin you use is suitable for the particular job you are doing. Resins for clear casting are especially made to remain clear with little or no optical distortion. They are also treated to avoid excessive shrinkage so that when a solid object is embedded in them they will not crack around the object. Polyester resin is easy to work with and is suitable for craft purposes in the home.

Terminology

A cast is the molded resin.

Pigments are special dyes used to color or tint the resins. They are either opaque or translucent.

Molds specially made for casting resin are available from craft shops in any size and shape, but you can improvise: any glass or metal container with a smooth, highly polished surface is suitable. Plastic molds or rubber molds can also be used but as the resin will react with polystyrene, containers made from this material are unsuitable. Generally, soft plastic molds such as polythene are safe, but the hard brittle types are not.

Curing is the hardening of the resin. This process starts once the catalyst has been added to the resin and is complete when the cast has set to a solid. Heat is generated during this process. Air inhibits the curing of a pour so the exposed surface of the cast remains tacky. You can overcome this either by covering the pour to expel all air, which is difficult, or by removing the tacky surface with acetone.

The catalyst is a chemical, usually a peroxide solution, which reacts with the resin to turn it into a solid.

Gel is the stage where the resin is set but not hard. At this stage the surface will appear slightly rippled and is ready for a second pour.

These paper weights and pen-holder are exceptionally fine examples of resin casting. The piece on the left has a graphic design on the base which is optically very effective. Supplied by Barnabas (Covent Garden) Ltd.

Steve Bicknell

Clear cast embedding

Embedding is the process whereby an object is placed within a solid mass of resin. This is usually done in two layers for a single object, or in a number of layers, depending on the number of objects and the way they are spaced. Each layer is known as a pour. The first pour is to create the outer surface and to support the object. The second pour is to cover the object, thus embedding it.

There is no end to the things that can be embedded in resin. The casts you make can be varied not only by the

Once the casts have cured they can be finished by gluing a design to the sticky surface. You can then attach jeweler's clasps to make pins, earrings and key rings.

To make clear cast objects you will need wooden stirrers, molds, paper cups, catalyst or hardener to mix with the resin, color pigments to tint the cast and a measuring cup.

object you embed but also by the shape of the mold and the color of the resin. You can tint the resin slightly for a special effect, or make the back or base of the mold an opaque color as a background for the object.

You can make paper weights, buttons, door knobs, jewelry, key rings, picture mounts, chess and backgammon pieces —in fact you can apply this technique to most objects.

Experiment with embedding dried flowers and grasses, some of which are more suitable than others. The color tends to fade—red more so than yellow —but everlasting flowers can be embedded successfully as they do not fade. You can embed coins, insects, colorful seeds, colored glass chips, watch parts, unusual stamps, address cards and shells. You can also make large clear blocks to mount photographs or to set photographs in. Remember that whatever you embed must be free of moisture.

The process is easy and you do not require any special tools. The materials are easily available and for a high gloss finish the cast can be polished with a metal polish. Resins can be purchased from hobby shops or manu-

facturers in various quantities. Buy the appropriate catalyst at the same time. You can buy an embedding kit or you can buy the resin and catalyst separately.

To make a cast

For example, a paper weight.
You will need:
Clear cast resin and catalyst
Mold
Object to embed
Waxed paper cups
Measuring cup, wooden stirrers
Wax polish
Optional—color pigment
Acetone is useful for cleaning, but it is highly inflammable so throw cleaning materials away.

Prepare your work area by covering the surface with paper.

Decide on the object you are going to embed, then select a mold suitable for the object's size and shape.

Measuring and preparing the mold. Some molds are marked with their capacity but, if not, fill mold with water up to the level required for the first pour—usually $\frac{1}{2}$-$\frac{1}{3}$ the total depth of cast. Pour the water into a measuring cup to find the capacity.

If you do not want to mix the resin and catalyst in the measuring cup, pour the water into a paper cup and mark the water level. Dry the mold and the paper cup thoroughly before adding the resin.

Polish the mold with wax polish. Although this is not essential, depending on the type of mold you use, it does help to release the cast. If you want to make more than one cast prepare the molds together.

Remember that the open end of the mold will usually be the back or bottom of the object you are making. The smooth inside surface of the mold will form the outside surface of the cast.

Measure out the resin and add the appropriate amount of catalyst. If you want to tint the cast, add the pigment before you add the catalyst and mix it well—stirring slowly to avoid trapping air bubbles.

☐ Once the catalyst has been added, stir the mixture slowly for a minute before pouring it into the mold.

☐ Set the mold aside on a level surface and cover it lightly with foil to prevent the surface from collecting dust. You can place the mold at an angle if you want a sloping surface. Leave the cast for about three hours or until it has gelled. The length of time can vary depending on the amount of catalyst used.

Embedding an object

☐ Some objects are inclined to trap air when being embedded. If you are using a coin, prepare it by pouring a few

Glass beads were used to create this mosaic pattern.

It is difficult not to trap air bubbles when embedding intricate pieces.

Air bubbles between the photo and the cast spoil the effect of this piece.

Too much catalyst has been used in this cast, causing it to crack.

drops of resin mixed with catalyst onto the face. Leave to set and place this side down on the gel before the second pour.

Address cards can be treated in the same way. Dried flowers should be immersed in resin before being embedded.

☐ Place the object upside down on the tacky surface of the first pour. If the object is very light in weight you can coat it with a clear plastic adhesive to keep it in position. Once this has dried, make the second pour.

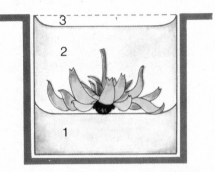

1. First pour 2. Object embedded in second pour 3. Resin or felt base.

☐ The sticky surface of the cast can be covered with a piece of felt or you can cover it with a thin layer of resin to which you have added more than the usual amount of catalyst. This will cure to a smooth finish.

The resin can take from 15 minutes to several hours to cure completely, depending on the brand of resin and the size of the cast.

Removing the cast. If a cast is difficult to remove from a mold, immerse it in cold water and bring to the boil. Then plunge it in cold water. If it still sticks repeat the process—it will work.

Polishing. Rub the cast down with a metal polish for a highly polished finish. You can also rub it down with a fine grade sandpaper and then use a metal polish, but this is difficult to do by hand and requires a lot of practice. If you do attempt it, try it out on a small test cast first.

Once you have made a few casts you will find it easy to make larger objects and to adapt the technique to a wide range of colorful articles.

Hints on embedding

Patience is essential for good results. Satisfy your initial enthusiasm by making small casts—larger casts take a long time to cure to obtain successful results. But even when making small casts, apply the following hints—they will improve your casts and make the whole process easier when you attempt larger pieces.

The object to be embedded must be dry and free of dust.

Avoid trapping air bubbles by stirring the resin slowly.

The percentage of catalyst used must be decreased as the amount of resin to be poured is increased. Too much catalyst will form cracks in the cast—although you might do this for special effects. The amount of heat generated is relative to the amount of catalyst used, so if an excessive amount of catalyst is used not only will it form cracks in the cast but it can also ruin the mold.

It is better to use too little catalyst than too much. The surface can always be cured artificially if necessary by applying a thin coat of resin to which a larger proportion of catalyst has been added. You can also use this method to glue a base to the tacky surface of the cast.

Store the resin containers in a cool, dark place and cover them so that they do not collect dust. Dust could fall into the resin when you pour it from the container, so work in a dust-free atmosphere and cover the casts while curing.

To avoid waste, always have a spare mold on hand in case you have any resin left over from a previous pour.

Barbara Firth

Safety hints

Be careful: some plastics can be inflammable, some fumes can be toxic, and some may irritate the skin. However, they are perfectly safe to work with in the home if you take the following simple precautions.

Store all plastic materials in a cool, dark place.

The room in which you are working must be warm and well ventilated.

Do not smoke when working with plastics and do not work in a room where there is an open flame.

Keep materials away from food.

Avoid contact with the eyes.

If you find it difficult to work wearing rubber gloves use a barrier cream on the hands.

Work on a heat resistant surface that has been covered with tinfoil or waxed paper.

Use disposable containers for mixing resin in and do not throw away the excess until it has cooled down.

Wear old clothing and remove any spilled resin with acetone.

Should your skin come into contact with the resin wash it immediately with cold water.

Wipe up any spilled resin with a paper towel and dispose of it—do not use it a second time.

Dispose of all cleaning materials and waste as soon as you have finished working with the resin.

Begin with granny squares

Crochet is quick and simple to work and, because it is so decorative, has become one of the most popular of all handicrafts. It is very adaptable and can be used in conjunction with many different fabrics and yarns. You can crochet borders, edgings and flower decorations which will enhance any garment; or you can create pictures, bedspreads and other home furnishings. The type of yarn used offers you as much scope as the articles you can make from it. Coarse wool or string can be made up into wall hangings or rugs while the finest yarns will make delicate table mats, fine curtains or gossamer-weight fabrics.

These chapters set out to explain the basic techniques so clearly that you will be able to make up any sort of

Bright and practical, this shoulder bag is just right for carrying those things a girl insists she cannot be without! The bandeau, which can be made in an evening even by a beginner, will keep your hair sleekly in place in most weathers and looks pretty too.

To make a chain

Make a slip loop at the end of your ball of yarn and place it on the hook.

Hold the hook in your right hand...

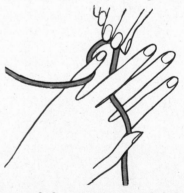

... and the yarn in your left hand, with the yarn looped around little finger. This loop helps to control the flow of yarn.

pattern to the size you require—and then go on to make up your own designs with your choice of yarn. The easiest way to learn to crochet is to begin by making small, manageable shapes like granny squares. Practice a square first using old scraps of sports yarn and a No. 4.00 ISR (U.S. size H) hook. These motifs are colorful and economical, since any odd scraps of the same thickness of yarn can be used and with the combination of triangles, you can produce a variety of shapes.

Slip stitch

Use it to join a new color: insert hook into stitch in previous row, make a loop with the new yarn, catch it around hook, pull through stitch, wind yarn and end around hook and pull through.

To join crochet pieces, match edges, insert hook through both thicknesses yarn around hook and draw loop through fabric and loop on hook in one movement.

This granny square uses three colors but when it gets bigger you can use more!

Wind the yarn around the hook once..

... and draw the yarn through the slip loop. One chain stitch has been made, leaving one loop on the hook —this is not counted as a stitch.

Continue making chain stitches in this way.

To work a double crochet

Make however many chain stitches you need and add 3 extra chain stitches. These make what is called a turning chain, which is required at the beginning of every row of double crochet to bring hook up to correct height to work the first stitch.

To work the first row, *wind the yarn around the hook, as shown for making a chain stitch and insert the hook from front to back into the fourth chain stitch from the hook, wind the yarn around the hook again ...

... and draw the loop through the chain stitch.

Wind the yarn around the hook ...

... and draw the yarn through 2 of the loops on the hook.

Wind the yarn around the hook and draw it through the remaining 2 loops on the hook.* One double crochet has been made, plus the first skipped 3 chain stitches which count as the first double crochet, leaving one loop on the hook. Repeat from * to * into next and every chain stitch to the end of the row.

On the next and every following row, turn the work so that the yarn is again in position for the beginning of the row. Make 3 chain stitches to count as the first double crochet, skip the first double crochet of the previous row, work one double crochet into each double crochet...

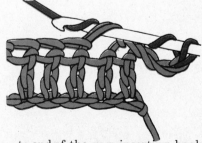

... to end of the row inserting hook under the top 2 loops of the double crochet in the previous row.

Granny square using one color.

Making a granny square

Using one color. Without breaking off yarn at end of each round. Make 6ch. Insert hook from front to back into first ch, yo and draw loop through ch and loop on hook in one movement. One sl/st has been worked to join ch into a circle.

1st round. 3ch to count as first dc, 2dc into circle working under ch, 2ch, work (3dc into circle, 2ch) 3 times. Join with sl/st to third of first 3ch.

The beginning of the second round.

2nd round. 2ch, work (3dc, 2ch, 3dc) into first 2ch sp to form corner, *1ch, work (3dc, 2ch, 3dc) into next 2ch sp,

rep from * twice more. Join with sl/st to first of first 2ch.

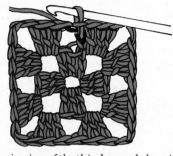

The beginning of the third round showing where the hook should be inserted.

3rd round. 3ch, 2dc into first ch sp to left of sl/st join of previous round, 1ch, *work (3dc, 2ch, 3dc, into 2ch sp, 1ch, 3dc into 1ch sp, 1ch, rep from * twice more, (3dc, 2ch, 3dc) into last 2ch sp, 1ch. Join with sl/st to third of first 3ch.

Working under the top two loops of the double crochet in the previous round.

4th round. 2ch, 3dc into next 1ch sp, 1ch, *work 3dc, 2ch, 3dc) into 2ch sp, 1ch, (3dc into 1ch sp, 1ch) twice, rep from * twice more, (3dc, 2ch, 3dc) into last 2ch sp, 1ch, 3dc into last 1ch sp. Join with sl/st to first of first 2ch. Break off yarn, draw end through loop on hook and draw up tightly—called 'fasten off'.

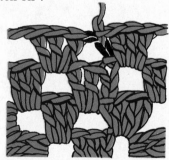

To fasten off, break the yarn and pull the end through loop on hook.

Granny squares using 2 or more colors. Breaking off yarn at end of each round. Make beginning ch and work first round as given for motif in one color. Break off yarn and fasten off.

2nd round. Join next color to any 2ch sp with sl/st, 3ch to count as first dc,

work 2dc into same ch sp, *1ch, work (3dc, 2ch, 3dc) into next 2ch sp to form corner, rep from * twice more, 1ch, 3dc into same 2ch sp as beginning of round, 2ch. Join with sl/st to third of first 3ch. Break off yarn and fasten off.

3rd round. Join next color to any 2ch sp with sl/st, 3ch to count as first dc, work 2dc into same ch sp, *1ch, 3dc into 1ch sp, 1ch, work (3dc, 2ch, 3dc) into 2ch sp, rep from * twice more, 1ch, 3dc into 1ch sp, 1ch, 3dc into same 2ch sp as beginning of round, 2ch. Join with sl/st to third of first 3ch. Break off yarn and fasten off.

4th round. Join next color to any 2ch sp with sl/st, 3ch to count as first dc, work 2dc into same ch sp, *(1ch, 3dc into next 1ch sp) twice, 1ch, work (3dc, 2ch, 3dc) into 2ch sp, rep from * twice more, (1ch, 3dc into next 1ch sp) twice, 1ch, 3dc into same 2ch sp as beginning of round, 2ch. Join with sl/st, to third of first 3ch. Break off yarn and fasten off. Darn in ends of yarn where colors were joined.

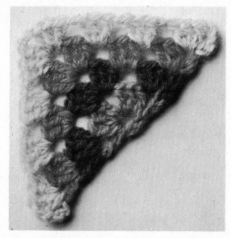

This triangle makes granny squares even more versatile.

To make a triangle

Using one or more colors. Breaking off yarn at end of every row. Make 5ch. Join with sl/st to first ch to form a circle.

1st row. Using same color, 4ch to count as first dc and 1ch sp, work (3dc, 2ch, 3dc) into circle, 1ch, 1dc into circle. Break off yarn and fasten off.

Each row must be started with a fresh strand of yarn from the same side at which the row was first begun.

2nd row. Join next color to third of first 4ch with sl/st. 4ch, 3dc into first 1ch sp, 1ch, work (3dc, 2ch, 3dc) into 2ch sp, 1ch, 3dc into last 1ch sp, 1ch, 1dc into top of last dc in previous row. Break off yarn and fasten off.

3rd row. Join next color to third of first 4ch with sl/st, 4ch, 3dc into first 1ch sp, 1ch, 3dc into next 1ch sp, 1ch, work (3dc, 2ch, 3dc) into 2ch sp, (1ch, 3dc into next 1ch sp) twice, 1ch, 1dc into top of last dc in previous row. Break off yarn and fasten off.

4th row. Join next color to third of

Chris Lewis

first 4ch with sl/st, 4ch, 3dc into first 1ch sp, 1ch, (3dc into next 1ch sp, 1ch) twice, work (3dc, 2ch, 3dc) into 2ch sp, (1ch, 3dc into next 1ch sp) 3 times, 1ch, 1dc into last dc. Break off yarn and fasten off.

Bandeau

For a bandeau 9cm (3½″) deep by 50cm (20″) long. Each motif measures 8cm (3¼″) square.
You will need:
50gm (1¾oz) of 4-ply yarn in 6 contrasting colors, ABCDE and F. If you use scraps of yarn, the size of the bandeau may vary.
One No.3.00 ISR (US size F) crochet hook
To work granny squares
Make 6 granny squares, using one or more colors as required.
Finishing
Sew squares tog and join into circle.
Edging. Using No.3.00 ISR (US size F) hook, any color and with RS of work facing, rejoin yarn with sl/st to any corner ch sp.
Next round. 3ch to count as first dc, (work 1dc into each dc and ch sp across top of first 3 squares), sl/st into same place as last dc, make 16ch, take ch down back of squares, around front to top again to gather the front, sl/st into next ch sp, 1dc into same place, work as given in parentheses across next 3 squares. Join with sl/st to third of first 3ch. Fasten off.
Work along other edge in same way omitting the 16ch loop.

Handbag

For a handbag 27cm (11″) square
Each motif measures 13cm (5½″) square
You will need:
50gm (1¾oz) of 4-ply yarn in main color and 100gm (3½oz) in 4 contrasting colors. If you use scraps of yarn, the size of the handbag may vary.
One No.3.00 ISR (US size F) crochet hook
To work granny squares
Make 10 granny squares using the colors as required.
Finishing
Sew 4 squares together to make a square, and sew the remaining squares together to form an oblong 27cm x 40cm (11″x16½″). Place the square against the oblong, WS together, matching the squares exactly. Sew around the 3 sides of the square and oblong where they meet. This forms the body of the bag with a flap consisting of 2 squares.
To work the handle
Make 152ch, work 1dc into every ch and work 6 rows, varying the colors as necessary.
To complete the bag
Sew the right sides of the 2 ends of the handle to the back of the bag just where it joins the flap. Lining the bag will increase its durability and help keep its shape.

Pillow

For a pillow 40cm (16″) square
You will need:
250gm (8¾oz) of yarn in one color
50gm (1¾oz) of sports yarn in each of 7 contrasting colors,
ABCDEF and G.
One No.4.00 ISR (US size H) crochet hook
Pillow form 40cm (16″) square
20cm (8″) zipper
To make large square
Using No.4.00 ISR (US size H) crochet hook and any color, work first 4 rounds as given for granny square, changing color for each round.
5th round. Join in any color with sl/st to corner 2ch sp, 3ch to count as first dc, 2dc into same sp, *(1ch, 3dc into next 1ch sp) 3 times, 1ch, (3dc, 2ch, 3dc) into corner 2ch sp, rep from * twice more; (1ch, 3dc into next 1ch sp) 3 times, 1ch; 3dc into same sp as beg of round, 2ch. Join with sl/st to third of first 3ch. Break off yarn and fasten off. Cont in this way changing the color as shown and working one more group of 3dc and 1ch on each side on every round until work measures 40cm (16″) across. Fasten off. Darn in all ends. Make another square in the same way.
Finishing
With RS of squares tog, join 3 edges. Turn RS out. Insert pillow form. Join rem seam, leaving sp to insert zipper in center.
Edging. Using No.4.00 ISR (US size H) hook and any color, rejoin yarn with sl/st to any corner sp through both thicknesses. Into each ch sp around all edges work (1sl/st, 4dc, 1sl/st) working through both thicknesses, except across zipper opening, where you only work through one thickness. Join with sl/st to first sl/st. Fasten off.
Sew in zipper.

Pillow made up in colorful sports yarn. Designer Pam Dawson.

Rupert Watts

39

Star weaving - God's eyes

A primitive form of weaving—star weaving—has in recent years found its way into contemporary decor. These colorful stars are most commonly seen in Latin America though they are also found in Africa and the East. In Latin America they are known as Ojos de Dios—God's Eyes. In Mexico God's Eyes were made to symbolize the eye of a god and were a supplication for help or watchful care from the gods. If more than one God's Eye was woven onto the crossed sticks then it was primarily for the gods to look kindly upon a child. A God's Eye was made for each year of a child's life up to five years—after this the child was supposed to be able to make his own requests. The age of a child could also be represented by the number of colors used.

Today God's Eyes are enjoyed for their use of color and texture and because they are easy and fun to make. The materials are inexpensive and readily available. This is an excellent opportunity to use up scraps of yarn.

Materials

You will need two straight sticks or dowels of about the same length and thickness. You can use sticks from the garden but straight, smooth sticks are the easiest to use to begin with.

When choosing yarn let your imagination run wild with color combinations. The thickness of the yarn should be relative to the thickness of the sticks. 6mm ($\frac{1}{4}$″) diameter sticks work best with sports yarn weight. With practice you will be able to vary the yarn weights on each project.

The yarn may be of any material—wool, cotton or man-made fibers. It is best to use at least 2-ply on your first projects as you will be pulling on it to maintain the tension.

To make a star

You will need:

2 sticks, each 28cm (11″) long and 6mm ($\frac{1}{4}$″) thick
3-ply rug yarn in following amounts:
orange — 15.5m (17yd)
purple — 14.5m (16yd)
red — 1m (1yd)
blue — 6.5m (7yd)
yellow — 2.75m (3yd)
rose — 14.5m (16yd)

Remember—it is always better to have too much yarn rather than not enough.

Lashing. Lay one stick on top of the other at right angles with centers matching.

☐ Lay one end of yarn (in this case orange) diagonally across the intersection of the two sticks.

☐ Hold the tail of yarn to the junction of the sticks with your thumb. At the same time, hold the junction of the sticks, on the side away from you, with the index and middle finger of the same hand.

☐ With your free hand begin winding the yarn away from you diagonally, holding it taut as you do so. In this way the yarn should cross the sticks diagonally at the junction, on one side and have parallel sides on the other.

☐ Wind the yarn diagonally around the crossing point of the sticks alternately to the right and to the left, thus forming an X over the center of the sticks (fig.1). When the center wood is

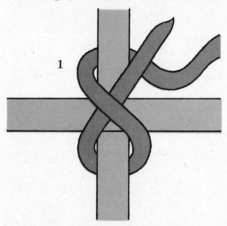

1. *Start the lashing by making a figure eight around the two sticks.*

totally covered, you have lashed the sticks together.

Note: remember to pull the yarn taut as you wrap so sticks stay in place.

☐ Turn the sticks over and tie a small but tight knot at the center of the back with the original tail of the yarn and the yarn you now hold in your hand. This secures the lashing. Do not cut the yarn. Turn the sticks over again so that the knot is at the back. The side facing you is from now on the 'right side' of the star. Always work with this side facing you.

Weaving. There are two basic methods of wrapping the yarn to make stars. One shows the shape of the sticks (fig.2), the other covers the shape of the sticks completely and is slightly raised (fig.3). In both cases, all wood is covered until the outer edge of the star is reached.

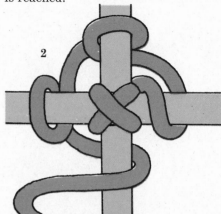

2. *The recessed method of wrapping.*

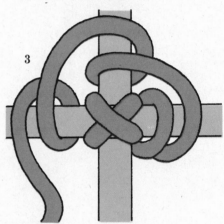

3. *This is the raised method of wrapping which covers the shape of the sticks.*

This example continues with the orange yarn that was used for the lashing, and begins with the method that covers the shape of the sticks completely.

☐ Begin by holding the star in one hand and the yarn in the other (with the right side of the star facing you).

☐ Carry the orange yarn over one stick so that the yarn lies just next to the last round of lashing.

☐ Bring the yarn under the stick and back around the top of the stick (fig. 3). (Keep the yarn taut throughout the entire procedure.) You have now completed one wrapping.

☐ Carry the yarn forward to the next arm of the star. Again, lay the yarn on top of the stick next to the last round of lashing. Wind the yarn under the stick and around the top of the stick. Don't forget to keep the yarn pulled taut.

☐ Continue on to the next arm of the star and finally the fourth arm and back to where you began. You have now completed one round. Repeat this round until you have woven about

2.5cm (1″) from the center of the star in each direction.

Changing colors. You are now ready to change colors. This design changes from orange to purple.

☐ On the wrong side of the star stop at one arm and cut the yarn leaving a tail of about 5cm (2″).

☐ Loop the tail once around the arm and tuck the end under the loop. Pull the end tightly. (This will hold the tension of the yarn in place while you join the new color.)

☐ Making a double knot, attach the purple yarn to the tail of orange yarn. Tie the knot as close as possible to the arm of the star (fig.4).

☐ Continue wrapping the purple yarn

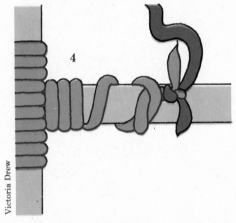

4. Join a new color on the wrong side of the stick with a tight knot.

around the arms of the star just as you did with the orange yarn.

To follow the example shown, wrap the purple yarn until its width is 12mm ($\frac{1}{2}$″).

☐ Change to the red yarn, following the method for changing colors. After winding the red yarn for 6mm ($\frac{1}{4}$″) in width, change to a blue yarn.

☐ With the blue yarn change to the other technique of wrapping the yarn (fig.2). You will note that the blue area appears to be recessed. This is due to the second wrapping technique which shows the shapes of the sticks.

☐ Begin by wrapping the blue yarn under the nearest arm of the star.

☐ Now bring the yarn around the top of the stick and around the underside again.

☐ Carry the yarn to the next arm and repeat the first two steps (fig.2). The blue yarn is wrapped for a width of 12mm ($\frac{1}{2}$″). Now, change back to the orange yarn and wrap it for a width of 6mm ($\frac{1}{4}$″).

☐ Then change to a yellow yarn and resume the original method of wrapping (going over the stick, then under and back over). Continue this method to near the end of the sticks. The yellow yarn is wound for a width of 6mm ($\frac{1}{4}$″). Then wind the rose yarn for 18mm ($\frac{3}{4}$″); purple for 12mm ($\frac{1}{2}$″); orange for

This star uses the raised method of wrapping broken by just a small area of the recessed method. The lower end, being longer, is covered by winding the yarn around and around. The star is light enough to be hung from a small nail hammered into a wall.

12mm ($\frac{1}{2}$″) and finally purple for 18mm ($\frac{3}{4}$″).

Finally, on the wrong side, knot the purple yarn with an overhand knot.

If you wish to cover the longer bottom arm of the star, as has been done in this model, do not cut the purple yarn close

to the knot after you have finished weaving the star, but instead wrap the yarn round and round the stick until you reach the end. Then make your overhand knot on the wrong side of the stick. This is a good method of covering the ends of the sticks that are longer than the others.

Finishing. Make certain that all knots are tight and cut tails close to the knots for a neat finish.

Decorating stars

You may leave your star as it is, or further embellish it with various orna-

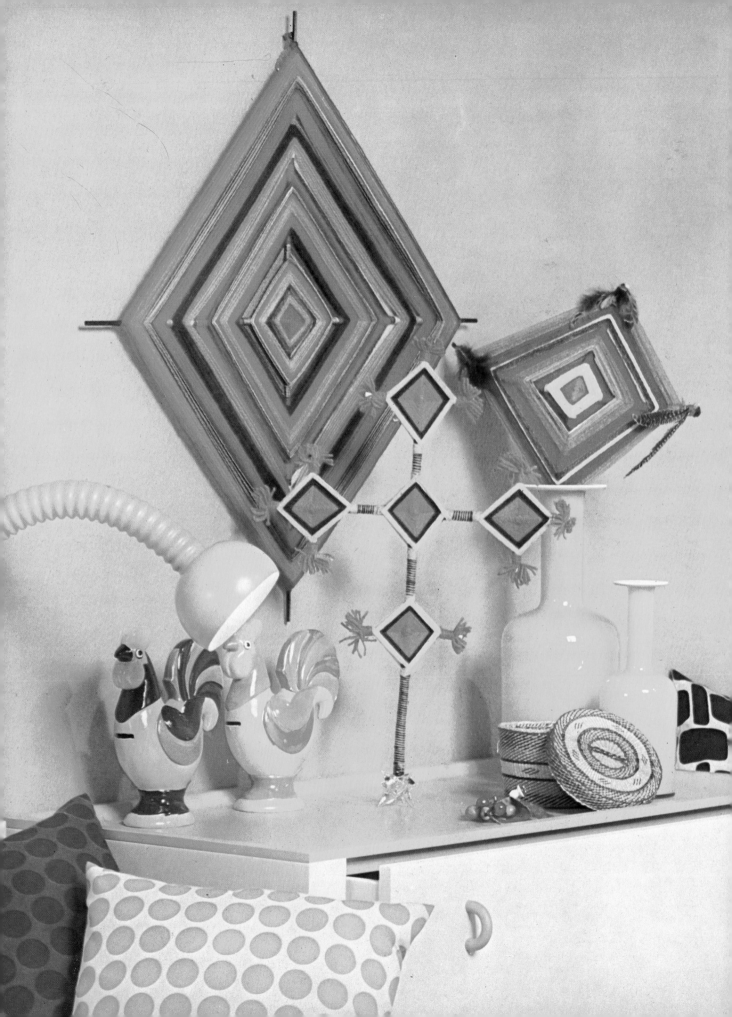

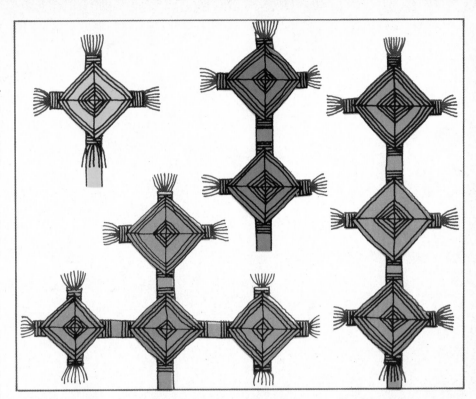

ments. The most common practice is to hang things from the exposed ends of the arms. You may, however, wish to sew or weave objects on to the face of the weaving. Tassels, pompons, feathers, bows, buttons, seashells and beads can all be used as ornaments.

As you become more proficient at making stars, you may want to try something more challenging. Some methods of varying stars are:

Irregular sticks will add bumps and concave areas to the wrapping. The sticks can be bumpy and/or curved to add interest. Just remember that these irregularities make it more difficult to maintain the tension and will require extra attention.

Very long, fat, short or thin sticks all give different looks to your stars. Remember that yarn thickness should be scaled up or down according to the size of the stick.

Besides changing colors with yarn, you may also like to try changing textures. There are all sorts of novelty yarns on the market, some giving a bumpy or looped effect. A smooth cotton followed by a bumpy, novelty yarn could give a dramatic effect.

God's Eyes

God's Eyes make a very effective hanging for a wall. Simply tie a string around the top arm, making a loop. Loop the string over a tack and you're all set. One star by itself looks good, or you may want to make a group of them, either all of one size or in a range of sizes.

Mobiles made with God's Eyes add a new dimension to a room. Children are attracted to them because of the lively colors.

You can even use very tiny stars (made with wooden tooth picks for the cross pieces and very fine wool or cotton) to hang on the Christmas tree. They add color in an original way.

Right: the very small stars are woven with very thin yarn on wooden tooth picks. The yarn is wrapped in the recessed method of under-over-under, described above. One star has plastic sequin birds attached to the ends of the arms, while another has buttons attached to the points.

The art of bead threading

The first steps in jewelry making are also some of the most exciting. With the basic threading and knotting techniques, and an understanding of the right threads and fastenings, a dazzling treasure chest of necklace designs opens up. It also means you can go through your jewelry box and either mend or restyle existing pieces.

Making your own necklaces is great fun and the results are, of course, unique and very personal—and also surprisingly inexpensive. But before you get carried away with enthusiasm, it's well worth learning the appropriate thread, closure and knotting technique for a well-finished, durable result. There's nothing more irritating than an unknotted thread breaking and showering beads all over the floor!

Most modern necklaces fall into one of three categories. First there is classic simplicity, reminiscent of traditional ropes of pearls—long strings of smooth beads à la 1920s, perhaps knotted at the bosom. Then there is the delicate look which uses sequins, tiny glass beads and mother-of-pearl. Thirdly there is an important trend towards the primitive, with hand-made, slightly uneven shapes, marvelously contrasting textures and bold use of color. Basic back-to-nature materials are much in evidence—wood, bamboo, metals, shells, clay, glass, bone, and even nuts, seeds, dried berries, animal and fish teeth, pieces of bone, scraps of leather and pieces of driftwood.

Where to find beads

Craft shops are Aladdin's caves for the jewelry maker, selling multicolored beads as tiny as hundreds-and-thousands or as large as golf balls; wooden balls, natural or dyed, and polished in a rainbow assortment of colors and just as many sizes; knobby textured, rough cut stones; bamboo and ceramics cut into macaroni shapes; glass beads—plain, iridescent or marbled, and disks made from clay, wood or—expensive but utterly ravishing—mother-of-pearl.

Some unusual glass beads which are inexpensive and easily obtainable:

'Eye' beads, which are still hand made in the Middle East, are believed to ward off the evil eye.

Rotelles are beads with large holes and look like round beads that have been patted flat.

Rocailles are the smallest of beads and come in a multitude of colors.

The model is wearing, from top: a choker of fish vertebrae with brown, round wooden beads; a plain necklace of round, creamy wooden disks; a chunky necklace of tiny cream and ox-blood wooden beads, interspersed with large polystyrene balls covered with beads. Designed by Karina Sterry.

Steve Bicknell

Bugle beads, thin and tubular, are often used in elaborate embroidery.

You can buy buttons and sequins from notions stores, and brass nuts and washers from hardware shops.

Don't forget junk shops and sales—secondhand clothes can provide antique buttons quite cheaply, and special stones or a pretty clasp can be salvaged from broken necklace pieces sold for a few cents.

Once you know how to drill holes, mold clay and work metal, the possibilities for making your own jewelry are boundless.

What thread to use

The thread must, of course, be fine enough to pass through the holes of your beads, but sufficiently strong to carry their weight.

Synthetic sewing thread is fine but tough—ideal for tiny beads. It comes in a wide range of colors and is best used in conjunction with a beading needle.

Linen carpet thread is thicker and stronger. It, too, comes in a good range of colors and is useful for slightly larger glass or ceramic beads and small light wooden beads.

Fishing nylon 0.2mm (5lb breaking strength) from sporting goods stores is good because it is almost transparent, but it is slippery and difficult to knot. Threading a needle and knotting are made easier if you first flatten the end of the nylon.

Foxtail is a strong, knitted metal thread useful for heavy, opaque beads such as marbled Venetian glass.

Shirring elastic can be bought in various thicknesses, usually only in black or white, and is particularly useful for bracelets without clasps, designed to be slipped over the hand. It is best used with beads with large holes so that the large knots can be hidden by pushing right inside a bead hole.

Leather is strong, chic and excellent for larger items. Rounded rather than flat thongs are easier to thread, but sometimes more difficult to obtain. They can be found dyed in a good range of colors and are rigid enough to thread without the aid of a needle.

Other useful yarns are bead silk, dental floss (obtainable from drug stores), strong twist thread, thin cords and macramé twine.

Threading

Long thin beading needles are useful for threading beads with small holes, but needles of different gauges can be used as long as the eye will pass through the bead.

Some threads are stiff enough to be passed through a bead without a needle and other threads can be dipped in glue or twisted with soap to stiffen the ends.

Beautiful beads—from top left to right: glass heart; small shaped glass beads; pear-shaped glass beads; blue glass luster; Venetian mosaic; bugle beads; lamb's eye; rocaille beads (in box); turquoise rotelles; sequins, brass nuts and washers; gilt half cups; brass pipe olives; two Indian gilt beads; fish vertebra; white tubular rotelles; disks cut from ostrich egg; brown ceramic bead; large and small square red wooden beads; round and tubular wooden beads; wooden washer; white, many-sided beads; bamboo beads; round, matt wood-grain bead; small, shiny wood-grain; unstained bead.

Alasdair Ogilvie

Bead knotting

You may want to use knots for a variety of reasons: to space out the beads for appearance's sake; to space them out in order to make them go farther; or to secure each bead, so that if the necklace should break, all the beads will not slide off.

The knotting methods depend on the relationship between the bead hole and the thickness of the thread.

Overhand knot. If you tie an overhand knot, as shown, will it be large enough to prevent the bead from sliding over it? You will only be able to find out by trial and error.

Overhand knot with double thread.

Double overhand knot. If you wish to knot the beads very closely, as for pearls, you will find it easier to make a fairly loose, double overhand knot, then ease it up to the bead with a needle, and pull it tight up against the bead.

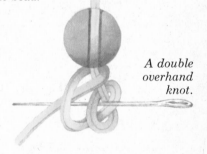

A double overhand knot.

Bead knot. If the thread is fine enough to pass through a small bead twice, you can string a small bead on each side of a larger one, passing the thread twice through the smaller beads.

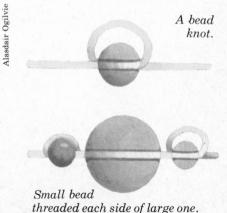

A bead knot.

Small bead threaded each side of large one.

Choosing a fastening

Rounded leather lends itself to the simplest fastenings of all—tie closure and pull closure, which need no clasps.

Tie closure. Check the beads are in the center of the leather, then fasten each end by making an overhand knot after the first and last bead. Leave 15cm (6″) then make another overhand knot, thread a single small bead, make a final knot and cut the leather. If the bead fits tightly the second knot can be omitted as illustrated.

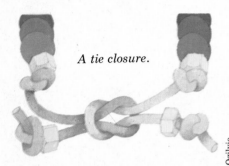

A tie closure.

Pull closure. When all the necklace beads are in position, thread both ends of the thong through a single, tightly fitting bead or washer. Leave 15cm (6″), then finish off each thong separately with overhand knots and a bead as described above.

A pull closure.

Button loop closures can be used on necklaces threaded onto synthetic or linen carpet thread. Finish off one end of the necklace with a well secured, large bead, and the other end with a series of smaller beads threaded to form a loop. Make sure the large bead will fit through this loop, then pass your thread through the loop beads a second time and secure by threading back and knotting through several inches of the necklace itself. Alternatively, glue the ends of the threads before passing them through the last bead. The glue will adhere to the inside of the bead and hold it securely out of sight. Use this method for finishing off thread ends.

A button loop closure.

Metal fastenings (or findings). Jewelers and craft shops supply traditional necklace clasps, bolt rings and screw rings. They may also stock closures commonly used on watch straps, and hook and eye fastenings in various sizes and different metals. Some findings have perforated surfaces so that smaller beads can be stitched on.

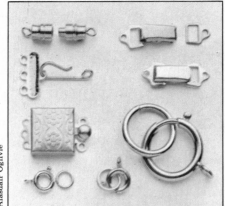

Metal fastenings—from top left to right; gilt screw clasp; gilt bracelet clasp (open); gilt hook and bar; nickel bracelet clasp (closed); gilt box clasp; large nickel bolt ring and jump ring; two small bolt rings and split rings.

Attaching findings

Bolt ring. Thread the yarn through the clasp eye. Tie an overhand knot with double thread next to the clasp. Tie the ends with a knot and snip neatly, so that, as beads are threaded, one of the beads hides the knot.

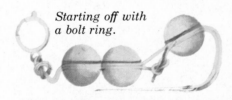

Starting off with a bolt ring.

Split ring. Finish off by looping the thread around the split ring, knotting and then re-threading the ends back through the last couple of beads.

Finishing off with a split ring.

Box clasps. For extra strength and a neat attachment, first loop the thread through one end of the clasp, then pass both ends of the thread through your needle and string the beads onto the double thread. After a necklace or bracelet is finished, take the thread ends under the tongue and the back of the clasp, and then take them up through the last two beads.

Washers and beads
You will need:
0.75m (28″) of round leather thonging
Sixty 12mm (½″) diameter brass washers
Four 18mm (¾″) round glass beads (2 yellow, 2 green)
Six 12mm (½″) round flat beads (orange)
Twenty-two 6mm (¼″) round beads (white)
Two 12mm (½″) long oval beads (black)
Two 3mm (⅛″) brass olives
One 6mm (¼″) brass olive
☐ Thread a white bead at one end of the thong and tie an overhand knot at each side to secure.
☐ Leave 15cm (6″) free for tying the necklace. Thread a black oval bead that fits tightly on the thong, or tie an overhand knot to hold the bead in place.
☐ Thread a white bead and 6 brass washers, then continue threading as in the picture, placing the large brass olive, flanked by the small brass olives, in the center.
☐ When the last black bead is threaded, finish off to match the other end.

Two strand necklace
You will need:
Two 1.25m (4′) lengths of linen thread
Blunt needle
Gilt box clasp with two or three attachments for thread
Twelve 6mm (¼″) wooden beads (lime)
Twenty 10mm (⅜″) wooden beads (lime)
Sixteen 10mm (⅜″) wooden beads (lemon)
18 x 12mm (½″) wooden beads (lemon)
132 brass cups
68 small brass or gold beads
☐ Attach one length of thread to the outside hole on the clasp, following the instructions above.
☐ Thread the beads as follows: brass bead, brass cup, 10mm (⅜″) lemon bead, brass cup, brass bead, brass cup, 6mm (¼″) lime bead.
☐ After the 7th wooden bead (4th lemon, 3rd lime), thread a 10mm (⅜″) lime bead, then a 12mm (½″) lemon.

Brass washer and bead necklace.

Continue threading, alternating the colors as before.

☐ After the eleventh large lime bead, thread the smaller beads as before.

☐ Fasten off in the outside hole of the other half of the clasp.

☐ For the inner strand, attach thread to the inner hole of the clasp. Work as before but with 9 large lime and 8 large lemon beads in the center. Fasten off in the inner hole of the other half of the clasp.

Glass luster necklace
You will need:
Gilt bolt ring with split ring
1.5m (5′) of linen thread (use double)
Blunt needle
27 10mm (⅜″) glass luster beads (blue)
106 brass half cups
52 brass beads

☐ Fasten the thread firmly to the bolt ring of the fastener.

☐ Thread as follows: brass cup, luster bead, brass cup, brass bead, two brass cups, brass bead, brass cup, luster bead.

☐ Continue to the end, attach split ring and fasten off thread.

Glass necklace
You will need:
60cm (2′) of foxtail or 1.25m (4′) of bead silk or strong thread (double)
Blunt needle
49 10mm (⅜″) Venetian mosaic beads

☐ Thread the beads and fasten off very firmly, pushing the knot back inside the bead and threading any excess back through two or three beads.

These beads are expensive, so it is a good idea to make a knot between each one for safety.

Red, white and blue
You will need:
Bolt ring with split ring
1.25m (4′) of thick linen thread (use double)
Blunt needle
Fourteen 6mm (¼″) tubes (red), 2.5cm (1″) long
Thirty 6mm (¼″) rotelles (white)
Fifteen 6mm (¼″) rotelles (dark blue)

☐ Fasten the thread firmly to the bolt ring of the fastener.

☐ Thread as follows: one white, one dark blue, one white, one red. Continue this sequence ending with one white, one dark blue, one white.

☐ Attach split ring and fasten off thread in the usual way.

Beads and brass nuts
You will need:
1m (1yd) of natural, round leather thonging
Twenty 18mm (¾″) shiny, large-holed wooden beads (dark green)
Twenty-three 6mm (¼″) brass nuts

☐ Thread the beads and nuts alternately. Make sure the beads are in the center of the thonging and knot closely

to each end bead. Thread a brass nut on each thong end, leave 10cm (4″) for tying and make another knot.

Lamb's eye necklace
You will need:
1m (1yd) natural, round leather thong
Six 18mm (¾″) shiny, large-holed wooden beads (dark green)
Fifty-eight 6mm (¼″) rotelles (light blue)
Five 12mm (½″) lamb's eye beads

☐ Thread 13 rotelles, one dark green bead, 3 rotelles, a lamb's eye, 3 rotelles and a dark green bead. Continue this pattern until the last green bead, then thread 13 rotelles.

☐ Make sure the beads are in the center of the thonging and knot close to each end bead. Leave 15cm (6″) free for tying, make a knot, thread the last rotelle at each end and knot again.

Left to right: two-strand lemon and lime necklace; blue glass lusters and brass necklace; Venetian glass beads; red, white and blue necklace; green bead and brass nut necklace; lamb's eye necklace; graduated wood-grain beads. Designed by Karina Sterry.

Long wood necklace
You will need:
3.5m (11′) linen thread (used double)
Blunt needle
Nickel screw clasp
Eighty 6mm (¼″) wood grain beads
Forty 10mm (⅜″) wood grain beads
25 16mm (⅝″) wood grain beads
Attach the thread to the screw fastening and thread forty 6mm (¼″) beads, twenty 10mm (⅜″), 25 16mm (⅝″), twenty 10mm (⅜″) and forty 6mm (¼″) beads.

☐ Attach to other half of fastening.

Hard edge designing

Hard edge painting is one of the easiest and most effective techniques for decorative painting. It is achieved by painting against strips of masking tape. When the tape is removed, a perfectly straight, hard edge remains. This process is excellent for all kinds of striped or abstract patterns. It is primarily useful for decorating walls, but the same technique can be used for applying designs to furniture, floors — even on suitcases.

Preparing the surface. It is vital to have the right surface to work on — it must be smooth, free from old flaking paint and solid, not papered, as the tape might peel the paper when it is removed. It is best to cover the surface first with a good quality emulsion or latex paint.

One important note: before masking out your design, stick a small piece of tape onto the surface in an inconspicuous place. Press it firmly, wait a moment, and peel it off. It should come away cleanly without ripping the paint. There are special low-tack tapes for paint masking which you should use. Ordinary masking tape is more likely to damage the paint. *Never use transparent tape:* it's particularly damaging to a painted surface.

Basic principles

Use a ruler and a pencil to mark all the design lines. A carpenter's square will be useful for marking right angles and a level for horizontal lines.

Stick the masking tape carefully along these lines, leaving any areas of light color unmasked so that they can be painted first.

Angled corners. Lay the masking tape from one side of the corner over that from the other side and trim if necessary. Make sure there is no gap.

Travel-worn luggage can be given a new ticket to fashion with a few carefully placed and colored stripes, using the principles of hard edge design and techniques described here.

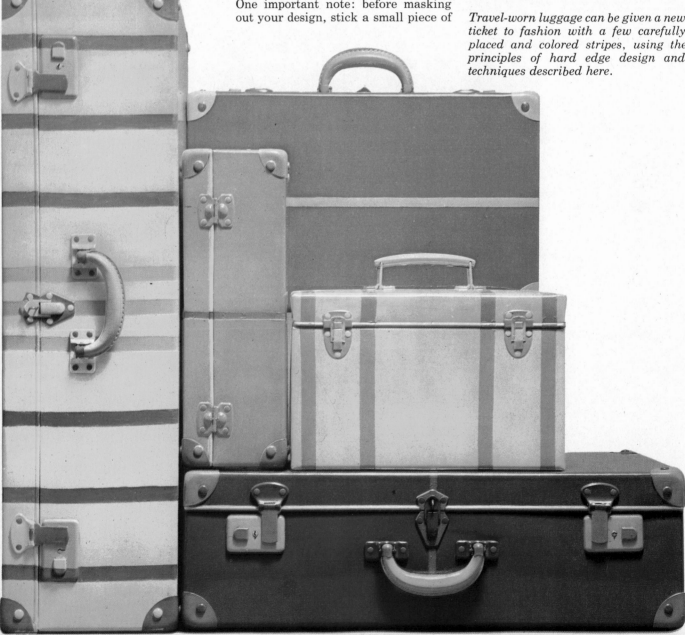

Rounded corners. Build up a solid square of tape over the whole corner. Using a compass, or string and pencil, draw the arc wanted (fig.1a). Cut carefully along this arc with a sharp blade and peel away the tape from the area you want to paint (fig.1b).

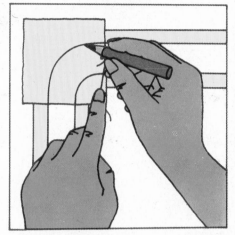

1a. *For rounded corners, draw an arc over the masking tape on each side of the stripe you are going to paint.*

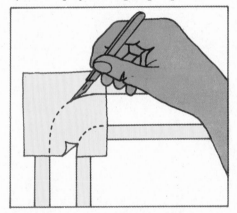

1b. *Cut along each arc with a sharp-bladed knife and peel off the tape covering where the stripe runs.*

From these basic principles you can create many different motifs. You can also use lines to accentuate an attractive window or break up a large wall.

Lighten your journey upstairs with broad bands of color that follow each bend and curve of the way.

A window that won't take curtains can be neatly covered in masked-off squares painted with gloss paint—and it won't cut off the daylight!

When you have finished masking, go over the whole area with a small wallpaper roller, or something similar, to make certain that the edges are firmly stuck so the paint cannot seep underneath. The longer you leave the tape the harder it sets, so paint as soon as you have fixed it. When the paint is touch-dry, carefully and slowly peel the tape off, lifting up the edge with a razor blade or sharp knife.

Suitable paints and brushes. If possible use sable brushes of a size appropriate to your design. For walls, a non-drip matt or eggshell emulsion paint is recommended as it should require only one coat. Use special floor paints, eg linoleum paint, for floors.

Painting the design. Remember that you paint the areas between the strips of tape and that sometimes, as with checks, you may need to wait for certain areas to dry before you can continue taping and painting adjacent areas.

Now that you know the basics of hard edge painting you could go the whole way and paint a complete wall with a tartan pattern!

Paint any areas of light color first and paint from top to bottom wherever possible. Make sure that this paint is absolutely dry before masking the edges to paint adjacent areas and always use fresh tape on a new area.

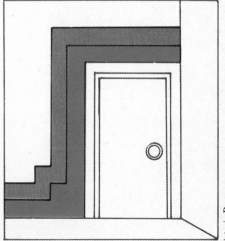

Lower a high ceiling and detail a door with hard edge stripes of color that tone in with your decor.

49

Bathrooms need not be boring if there is a clever use of color and shapes, not only in the ornaments you use but also in what you paint on the walls.

Pyramid frieze

Before starting to make this design based on an equilateral triangle (where each side is equal to the base), measure the width of your wall or the surface to be painted, and decide how many triangles you want and what size they should be. In the design illustrated there are 3 complete triangles across

the width, with a ½-triangle at each end. Each of their sides is ¼ the width of the wall. If you want 5 triangles, counting the 2 ½-triangles as one, their sides should be 1/5 the width of the wall, and so on.

☐ To make the basic shape of the design, draw an equilateral triangle whatever size you have decided. Do this on a piece of paper first before attempting to draw it on the wall.

☐ Divide the base of the triangle into 6 equal parts. Using these points, construct two more equilateral triangles

as shown (fig.2).

☐ Begin marking the front series of triangles on the wall, starting with the ½-triangle at one end (fig.3 ABC). The bases of the triangles should just touch to form a straight line, ending with another ½-triangle at the other end to complete the front row.

☐ To draw the back series of triangles follow exactly the same principle, only terminate the sides of the triangles where they meet the sides of the front series. Therefore, draw an equilateral triangle (fig.3 GBD), but don't draw in the dotted lines. The mid-point of the base of this triangle is where the front triangles touch.

Continue marking off points along the bases of the triangles and drawing in lines as in Fig.2. Repeat throughout the design.

☐ When you have drawn the whole design in this way, use masking tape to mask off each area of color in turn, as described above. Make sure when painting that each color is completely dry before you start to paint the color next to it.

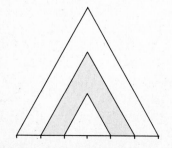

2. *The basic shape of this design is three equilateral triangles.*

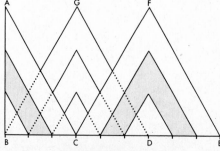

3. *Draw the whole design with the triangular motif repeated.*

Chevron design

When painting patterns such as this, where bands of different colors overlap, arrange the work so that you begin by painting the lightest colors. Draw the design on paper first to decide on your color scheme—experiment with different colors and shapes to make a variety of designs.

☐ To make the design illustrated, draw a square to the size required. This forms the outer boundary of the design. Divide each side into 16 equal segments. Draw an inner square as shown

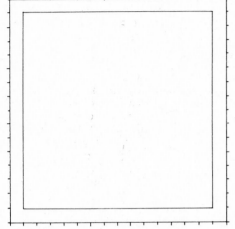

4. *Mark off the boundary square.*

(fig.4). All the diagonal lines of this design stop at the inner square. As this boundary will be black, do not paint it yet—it will cover any imperfections at the ends of the colored bands.

☐ To draw the white stripes, draw lines connecting the points marked on the outer square (fig.5). The dotted lines need not be drawn in.

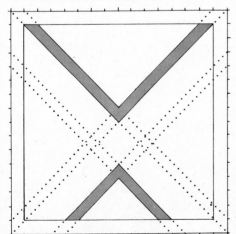

5. *Connect the outside points to give the white stripes (shaded gray).*

☐ Paint the shaded areas in white at this stage. If you have a friend to help you, you can check the positions of the stripes with string held taut between the marked points, and then lay the masking tape straight down. Check the position of the tape before you start to

paint—and remember to make sure that the edges are well stuck.

☐ To draw the light gray stripes, connect the points marked as before (fig.6). Where the lines intersect a stripe you have already painted, remember to lay masking tape over it. Paint in the shaded areas.

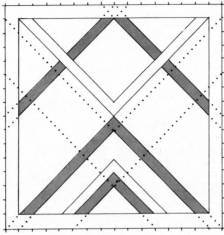

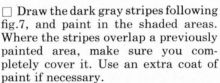

6. *Draw in the light gray stripes, which are shaded gray.*

☐ Draw the dark gray stripes following fig.7, and paint in the shaded areas. Where the stripes overlap a previously painted area, make sure you completely cover it. Use an extra coat of paint if necessary.

☐ Draw the black stripes following fig.8 and paint in the shaded areas.

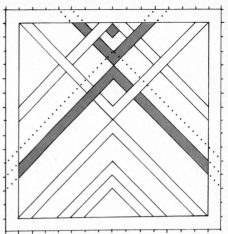

7. *Draw in the dark gray stripes.*

8. *Black stripes complete the design.*

Paint a rug on your floor if you're not fond of carpets or plain boards.

Maison de Marie Claire/Galland

Dipped and rolled candles

The very first candles probably consisted of pine branches, saturated either naturally or artificially with resin or fat. Sketches on prehistoric cave walls and ancient Egyptian tombs illustrate the use of candles and Pliny, in the first century AD, reported that in his time candles in Greece and Rome were made from flax threads coated with pitch and wax. During the Middle Ages the poorer folk burned tallow, the rich—beeswax. The Roman Catholic churches actually demanded that their candles be made with a very large percentage of beeswax and even today they must still contain 25% beeswax.

As well as providing light, another primary use for candles was to act as a clock. King Alfred the Great and his subjects were able to tell the time of day from candles that burned a certain, marked-off section in an hour. And right up until this century, bidding times at auctions were limited by means of a pin stuck into the side of a candle; proceedings stopped as soon as the pin fell out.

Beeswax and tallow were the only solid materials used in candlemaking until the end of the 18th century when the Sperm Oil Fishery began producing spermaceti, which yielded candles of great beauty, light—and expense! However, with the large-scale discovery of crude petroleum in 1859, paraffin wax emerged as a candle-making material and has prevailed ever since.

All the materials and equipment you will need to make the candles shown here are listed below. Collect together everything necessary before you start work. Some things you will already have around the house the rest are available from candlemakers' suppliers or drug stores. Some suppliers produce a special beginner's kit to start you off.

Materials

Paraffin wax is available in solid blocks or in powdered form, ranging from pure white to cream. The grades vary widely but, for most candles, it is best to use a fully refined wax with a melting point of 57°C-60°C (135°F-140°F). The powdered paraffin wax is the simplest to use. You can also melt down old candle stubs and even your own failures. Plain-colored pieces are easy to melt but if they are multi-colored you will have to try to break up the component parts and melt them separately or you will end up with murky, brown candles.

Beeswax. You can buy this either in blocks or in honeycombed sheets of about 20cm x 40cm (8"x16"). Beeswax is expensive, so it's a luxury to use it alone—the best method is to add a little to paraffin wax. This will give your finished candle a superior gloss and will also make it burn longer.

The sheets come in natural and in several other colors and can be used alone to give rolled, honeycomb-effect candles. You will get about two large candles from each sheet. Any left-over scraps of beeswax sheet can be melted down and added to ordinary paraffin wax in the normal way.

Beekeepers, after they have removed their honey, can melt down the rest in boiling water. When it cools, the dross will have settled on the underside of the resulting cake of beeswax and can be scraped off so that the wax can be used.

Stearin. This is a white, flaky type of wax which helps dye to dissolve easily and completely. Stearin makes candles opaque (both pure white as well as colored ones) and it is the stearin which causes the wax mixture to shrink a little and slip out of its mold easily. Use it in the proportion of 10% stearin to 90% wax.

Wax dyes. It is best to use these special dyes for candlemaking as opposed to any other kind of coloring. They are available in either powder or solid disk form and it is essential to take care when adding them to the wax —too much dye will mean that your candle will not glow.

Test the strength of the dye by taking a spoonful of the colored candle wax and dropping it into cold water; as it sets, you will get an idea of the depth of the color. So start with a little dye and build up the strength if necessary. For most colors a tiny pinch of powdered dye will color 0.5lit (1pt) of liquid wax. The solid disks will each color 2kg (about 4½lb) of wax to a pure, strong shade. If you want a lighter color, cut the disk to size; if you want it darker, use more dye. You can also mix the colors so that you can choose from a much greater range. Powdered dye is cheaper but the disks give you a greater degree of accuracy.

Wicks. Candle wicks are made of bleached, woven linen thread and are usually sold in packs, sized according to the diameter of candle they will successfully burn. A 2.5cm (1") wick will burn a paraffin wax candle 2.5cm (1") in diameter. It will also burn a 2.5cm (1") diameter hole in a larger candle so it is essential to choose the correct size, otherwise your wick could drown in a pool of molten wax. Likewise, a 5cm (2") wick in a 2.5cm (1") candle will burn down in no time.

Barbara Firth

Equipment

Thermometer. A candle thermometer with temperature readings up to 205°C (400°F) is essential. While there is very little danger of overheating wax to the point where it will burst into flames, it is impossible to judge when the wax is at the correct temperature without a thermometer. Also, each different type of candle—molded, sand or dipped—requires a different working temperature.

Don't leave your thermometer in setting wax and, if any wax sets hard, don't try and pick it off—you will break the thermometer; dip it in hot water and melt the wax off.

Pans and pitchers. Large pans are essential. Although you can manage with one by melting the stearin and dye first, then adding the wax, it is easier to dissolve the stearin and dye in one pan and melt the wax in another, especially if the wax is in block form and not powdered.

You need two tall pitchers (enamel is best), deeper than the length of the

Dipping can produce candles of varying thickness—tapers to chunky candles. Those shown here are 25mm (1") in diameter—the standard size for most candlesticks and holders. Designed by David Constable.

Graham Henderson

finished candle: one for dipping the candles and one for plunging them into cold water to harden.

Dipped candles

You will need:

1kg (2¼lb) paraffin wax
100gm (about ¼lb) stearin
Wax dye
Wick
Pan
2 tall pitchers
Thermometer
Stick or pencil
☐ Melt 100gm (about ¼lb) stearin and

sprinkle a little powdered dye or scrape some solid dye onto it. Keep on a gentle heat and stir until all the dye is completely dissolved.

☐ In another pan melt 1kg (about 2¼lb) paraffin wax.

Never heat wax over a fierce flame and be careful not to overheat, not to over-fill the pan and not to splash hot wax either on yourself or the stove—it will react in just the same way as hot fat. In the very unlikely event of your managing to overheat the wax beyond its flash point, turn off the flame and try to cover the pan (with its lid if

The pear was made by dipping progressively less and less of the candle so that it became fuller toward the bottom. It was then molded by hand when a little cooler and, when hard, the characteristic brown shading was painted on. All the other candles were overdipped to a different color, then plunged into cold water for a glossy shine. Designed by David Constable.

possible)—don't attempt to carry it!
☐ Add the wax to the stearin/dye mixture and heat to 82°C (180F°).
☐ Fill a pitcher with wax. Tie one end

54

of the wick length to a small stick or pencil and dip the wick into the wax. Remove it, pull it straight and hold it in the air for about 30 seconds until the wax hardens.

☐ Dip again and again until the candle is the right thickness for the wick (fig.1). Then hang it up to harden naturally.

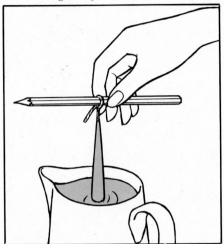

1. Tie the end of the wick to a stick or pencil and dip it into the hot wax. Pull it so that the waxed wick hardens straight, then continue dipping until the candle is the required size.

The wax in the pitcher may cool before the desired thickness is reached; bubbles appearing on the surface of the wax or on the last layer on the candle show that the wax has cooled. When this happens, re-heat the wax to 82°C (180°F) before you dip again.

Depending on how wide a neck the pitcher has, you can dip more than one candle together. Plunge the finished candle into a tall pitcher of cold water.

Variations

Shaping. Candles can be molded to shape between dips. Build up the candle to about 12mm ($\frac{1}{2}$″) in diameter, then dip progressively less of the candle in the wax from a quarter of the way down the candle only, so that the lower part begins to thicken. At this stage roll the

Candle dipped in layers, hand-molded into a ball and sections carved out.

candle between your hands to the shape you want. A pear-shaped candle can be made in this way.

Carving. By dipping a length of wick into a succession of different colors and building each one up to about 6mm ($\frac{1}{4}$″) thick, you can form multi-colored layers. For this process, the wax must be very strongly dyed or the layers of color will show through each other. When the candle is quite cold, carve patterns in the wax to reveal the underlying colors.

Twisting. To twist a dipped candle, take one that is still soft, lay it on a clean, smooth surface and flatten it slightly with a rolling pin. If it sticks, slide a knife under it and turn it over. Tap the base gently to square it off, then turn one end one way and the other end in the opposite direction at the same time to make the twist along the entire length of the candle. Cool it immediately in cold water.

Leave the candle in cold water until it is completely hard. Wax takes a long time to cool and if you take it out before it is really cold, the candle will distort.

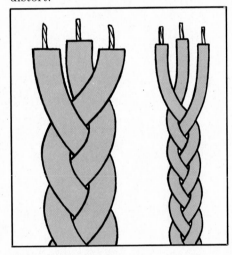

Braiding a candle.

Braiding. A braid of three different colored dipped candles can be made very simply if you have someone to help you. Get them to hold the three ends as you braid while they are still soft and pliable. Cool at once in cold water.

Rolled beeswax

This traditional method of candle-making uses sheets of pure beeswax, honeycomb-textured and smelling delightfully of honey. As the sheets are usually workable at room temperature, you can roll a candle quite easily in a few minutes without heating. In colder weather you may have to soften the sheets slightly by warming them by a heater for a few minutes.

Choose a suitable wick for the finished diameter of the candle and cut it to the required candle length, plus a little

extra. Lay the wick along one edge of the sheet (fig.2) and fold the wax over

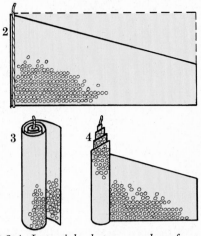

2,3,4. Lay wick along one edge of beeswax sheet (the longer edge if you taper sheet) and roll up as shown.

to cover it. Roll up the candles gently and evenly, making sure that the base of the candle is level (fig.3). Press the edge gently against the rolled candle to prevent it from unrolling. Trim the wick to 6mm ($\frac{1}{4}$″) and dip the end of it in molten beeswax to prime it.

A variation can be made by trimming off the top end of the beeswax sheet at an angle (fig.2). Beginning at the longest side of the remaining section, lay the wick and roll up as before (fig.4).

Pieces of left-over beeswax can be used to decorate rolled candles. You can use two tapered sheets of different colors to give a two-tone effect.

Left to right: twisted dipped candle; squat bought candle, overdipped in yellow; red overdipped candle; brown overdipped candle; rolled beeswax.

Rectangles and triangles

There are several short-cuts to drawing approximate geometrical shapes by tracing around objects. You can, for example, use books to make quick rectangles, or use an artist's triangle for standard triangles. You will, however, often need to make exact geometrical figures. Here is a reminder of some ways to draw accurate squares, rectangles, triangles and diamonds.

Squares and rectangles

To make a square, draw a right angle (Design Know-how 1, page 28) with arms longer than the sides of the square (fig.1). Set the span of your compass to the length of the side of the square, put the pin at the right angle and draw arcs to cut both arms of the right angle. With the same span, put the pin at the points where the arcs cut the lines and draw two more arcs. Where these arcs intersect is the fourth corner of the square.

To make a rectangle, mark off the two sides of the rectangle along the arms of a right angle. Draw arcs from the end of each side marked, setting the span of the compass to the length of the other side. Where these arcs intersect is the fourth corner of the rectangle (fig.2).

Triangles

Triangles are useful for patchwork, for geometric designs in jewelry and hard edge painting. A triangle with all sides equal is an equilateral triangle and one with 2 sides equal is an isosceles triangle. A right angled triangle has one angle of 90°.

Make a right angled triangle by measuring off the required length of two sides of the triangle along the arms of the right angle (Design Know-how 1, page 28), then join these two points to create the third side of the triangle (fig.3).

For an isosceles triangle use a compass or the string and thumb tack method used in Design Know-how 1. Draw a straight line AB, which will be the base, and set the span of the compass or string to the length you want the two equal sides to be. With the pin at A and B in turn, draw two arcs to intersect at C. Join AC and BC to give the triangle (as pictured below in figure 4).

An equilateral triangle is a special kind of isosceles triangle, in which you set the span of the compass or string to the measurement AB when drawing the arcs. Construct in the same way as for an isosceles triangle (fig.5).

Diamonds made up from equilateral triangles fit neatly together to form patterns suitable for patchwork.

Diamonds

You can use two isosceles triangles to make diamond shapes. Place the triangles base to base: the resulting diamond shapes will vary according to the shapes of the triangles you use (fig.6).

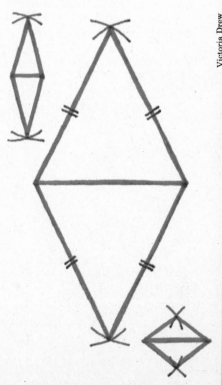

Victoria Drew

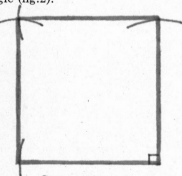

1. Constructing a square.

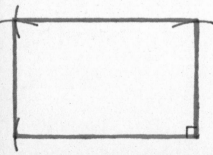

2. Constructing a rectangle.

3. A right angled triangle.

5. An equilateral triangle.

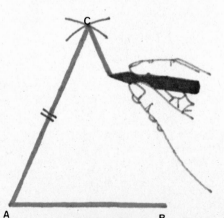

4. Drawing an isosceles triangle.

6. Two isosceles triangles, base to base, make a diamond shape.

Creative ideas 2

Above: brighten up your desk with colorful pencils, pots and mugs.

Left: cover cosmetic pots, glass jars, perfume bottles.

Below: put appropriate fruits on jam pots; decorate a set of storage jars or re-use discarded glass jars.

Chris Lewis

Although decorating everyday things with decals is not exactly a craft, it is an entertaining and artful way of making everyday objects more attractive. We buy a great many products in plastic or glass containers that are used regularly for months—and it is a lot more pleasing to eat jam or honey out of a pretty jar, or to keep bath oil or salts in a flowery bottle, than it is to face impersonal mass-produced packages every day. Most adhesive brand labels can be removed by soaking the container in warm water until the paper lifts off, or

they can be peeled off like transparent sticky tape. Some cartons have the brand name printed directly onto plastic and this can usually be rubbed off with a cloth or paper towel dipped in nail polish remover. This treatment also helps to remove the sticky film left by adhesive labels. Before applying a decal make quite sure that the surface is clean and free from grease. Decals usually come in sheets, so cut out the one you wish to use and soak it in warm water until the design loosens on the backing paper. Place the paper

in position and, holding the design in place with one hand, gently pull the backing sheet downward leaving the design in position. At this stage the decal is still wet enough to slide around if you have to adjust the position. Smooth out any water or air bubbles with a tissue or soft cloth and allow to dry in position. If you want to change the design, the decal can be removed by soaking in warm water until it lifts off. If you wish to make the design more permanent (and waterproof), allow the decal to dry and then paint over

the surface with a thin coat of clear polyurethane varnish. But remember that you should not eat or drink from a polyurethane varnished surface. Decals can be applied to almost any smooth surface and can be smoothed around corners and curves as long as you treat them carefully. In fact it is easy to become carried away with the speed and simplicity of the whole operation and cover every available surface with decals. So do plan your scheme in advance—pink roses for cosmetics and fruits for jam jars.

Pop-up cards using cut-outs

The cards shown here are a more sophisticated version of the pop-up principle described in Paper chapters 1 and 2. The pop-up shape is fixed by two tabs to the body of the card and folded away from the card. The pop-up can be any shape you wish—it can be an illustration cut from a magazine or book, or your own painting or drawing.

To make the basic pop-up

Using the same paper as the main card, cut out two tabs and stick them to the sides of the pop-up, as near to half way up as possible. If the tabs are placed too low, the pop-up will tilt forward, and if too high it will tilt backward. The tabs should also hinge as near as possible to the widest points of the pop-up; if they are not hinged from the widest point they should extend past it. So positioning them correctly is a question of balancing these requirements.

Fix the pop-up in position by slipping the tabs through two vertical slits cut in the card and taping or gluing them at the back. The position of the vertical slits can be determined by measuring the pop-up—the distance between the inside crease and the vertical slit should be the same as the corresponding opposite side of the pop-up (fig.1 where A=D and B=C).

If the cut-out shape is from a magazine or newspaper and is rather flimsy, it may be necessary to glue it first to a piece of paper to give it body. The paper needs to be dark so that the print on the other side of the pop-up does not show through. Use rubber cement rather than a water paste as it will not smudge the type.

All the cuts made here can be done with scissors, but the vertical slits are most easily made with an artists' knife and metal ruler.

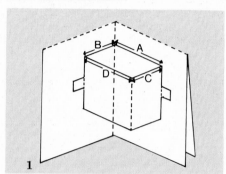

1

Chris Lewis

To make the jack-in-the-box card

You will need:
Dark brown construction paper, measuring 24cm x 52cm (9½″ x 20″)
Magazine picture of jack-in-the-box, or similar, measuring about 22cm x 10cm (8½″ x 4″)
Scissors, ruler
Rubber cement

☐ Fold the brown paper in half and in half again to make 26cm x 12cm (10″x 4¾″). Crease the pop-up shape sharply

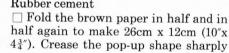

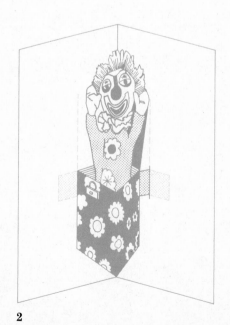

2

in half. Find a point half way up the card and decide on the relation between this point and where the pop-up shape is widest. In the case of the card shown here, the central point on the left side of the card coincides with the widest point of the pop-up at the top edge of the box, so the pop-up hinge is flush with the edge of the pop-up itself.

☐ On the right hand side, the widest point of the pop-up is the tip of the fingers, so the tab extends to this width before being inserted into the slit (fig.2).

☐ Cut two tabs from dark brown paper, 6cm (2½″) long and 2cm (¾″) wide. Glue or tape them to the back of the pop-up shape. Measure side C of the pop-up, from center crease to tab hinge. Mark a point on side B this distance from the center crease. Repeat with sides A and D, remembering in this case that the tab hinge is parallel with the widest point of the pop-up, the fingers.

☐ Open up the card and cut two vertical slits at these points, to the same depth as the width of the tabs. These slits can be cut with small, pointed scissors.

☐ Carefully slide the tabs through the slits, and glue or tape them to the back of the card.

Right: a cut-out butterfly is another variation on the pop-up theme. Add some flower decals to complete.
All cards designed by Joanna Ball.

To make the heart card

You will need:
Lilac construction paper measuring 35cm x 18cm (14″x7″)
Paper doily, with a solid center 10cm (4″) in diameter
10cm (4″) squares of red and brown gummed paper
Cut-outs such as cupid, hands and flowers, all with tabs added to the sides
A compass, scissors, ruler
Rubber cement

☐ Fold the lilac paper in half and in half again to make 17.5cm x 9cm (7″x3½″).

☐ Keeping the solid circle at the center, cut a rectangle 14cm x 15cm (5½″x 6″) from the doily. Spread glue over the center circle and dot it over odd points on the paper lace, paying particular attention to the edges. Stick the doily centered inside the card as shown (fig.3).

☐ Open out the card and, on the reverse of the side with the doily on it, mark a point on the crease line 4.5cm (1⅞″) up from the lower edge.

☐ With this point as the base and with the center crease as the center line draw a heart 7.5cm (3″) deep (fig.4).

☐ Refold the card in half lengthways and cut around the top end of the heart through both thicknesses, to the point where the arc joins the tangent.
Fold the heart over from this point to the base of the heart (figs.5a,b). Work crease to and fro several times.

☐ Refold the card, and ease the pop-up into position. Stick the square of brown gummed paper behind the heart on the inside of the card and cover the heart with red gummed paper.

☐ Fold the cupid shape in half vertically. Open up, and dab the side edges with glue. Lay the card flat and position the center crease of the cupid over the center crease of the card, inside the area covered by the heart but high enough for the cupid to be seen when the card is opened up. Stick down. Repeat this process with the cut-out joined hands and flowers shapes to complete the card.

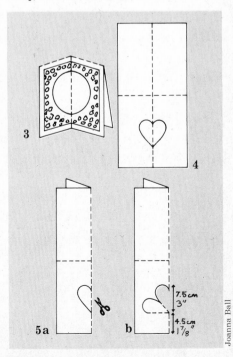

Surface designs on clay blocks

The block is one of the simplest shapes that can be made in clay. Both natural and self-hardening clays can be either pressed and patted into shape using a flat piece of wood or an old butter pat, or sliced with a cutting wire. Using a wire gives accurate shapes for jewelry, models and larger objects.

Simple blocks

Dice can be made very simply by pinching off lumps of clay about the size of a pingpong ball, rolling them into a smooth ball in the palms of the hands, then patting them into a cube shape against a flat surface (fig.1). The shape is finished off with a ruler or butter pat (fig.2). Once the block is complete, impress the groups of numbers with the end of a ball-point pen cap.

Cutting wire

A cutting wire is one of the potter's basic tools: the wire slices the clay to give a neat, straight edge, so it is particularly useful when working with the essentially geometric block or slab. To make a cutting wire, you will need a length of nylon bead thread or fishing line, about 33cm (13″) long and two duffle coat toggles or medium size buttons. Wind the end of the nylon thread around each toggle and tie with a slip knot, or secure a button at each end.

Decorating blocks

Once shaped, the block has great decorative potential—it can be impressed into, painted or modeled upon.
Impressed patterns. Impressed designs must be worked before the clay dries out. The decorating on these houses is done with a selection of 'tools'. Potters' wooden tools are cheap to buy, but it is just as simple to improvise with objects such as nails, sticks and knives, or whatever is at hand in the kitchen or workroom.
Using paint. Once the piece is complete, the clay must be left to dry out very slowly. Self-hardening clays, in particular, have a tendency to warp as they dry, so cover the work with a piece of plastic sheeting and expose it to the air very slowly.
When the clay is completely dry, it can be painted with poster paints, gouache, or India inks. Apply a base coat of color and let it dry very thoroughly before applying the contrasting decorative colors.
Modeling. Relief decoration can be added by rolling out a long, thin coil which is then stuck to the object to be decorated. If you are using natural clay, use a mixture of clay and water as the 'glue'. For self-hardening clay, thoroughly moisten the back of the coil and the tile surface and press the two together with the fingertips.

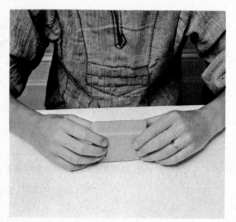

1. *Pat the clay into a rounded rectangular shape by tapping all the sides in turn against a flat surface.*

2. *Finish the squaring off process by tapping all the sides with a flat piece of wood or a butter pat.*

3. *Mark the line of the cut with a sharp knife and a ruler.*

4. *Use the cutting wire, held taut, to cut sharply through the clay along the guide line.*

5. *You may need to turn the block over when making the cut in order to draw the cutting wire cleanly through.*

6. *The clay block should not be too thick or it will warp when drying.*

Nelson Hargreaves

To make the houses

The houses shown are about 8cm x 5cm (3"x2"). To make 2 houses:

You will need:
About 250gm (½lb) clay
Cutting wire
Tools for impressing
Poster paints and brush for decorating
Varnish if required

☐ Make a rectangular block shaped in the same way as the dice, then slice it with the cutting wire. Use a ruler and sharp knife to mark the lines to be cut (fig.3), in this case the gable ends of the house.

☐ Hold the wire very taut between the thumb and fingers of both hands and draw it down firmly through the clay to make the cut (figs.4,5).

☐ Check that the bottom is straight so that the house will eventually stand on end. If it is not straight, tap the base of the house against a flat surface until the bottom is leveled off.

☐ The finished clay piece should not be too thick or it will not dry satisfactorily, so cut in half any piece more than 4cm (1½") thick (fig.6).

☐ Either impress patterns before the clay dries or paint and varnish when completely dry.

The blue houses are painted with a base coat of strong color, after which the contrasting windows and other decorations are applied.

Modeled pins

To make a pin about 5cm (2") wide
You will need:
Lump of clay about the size of a ping-pong ball
Poster paints and brush for decorating
Varnish if required
2.5cm (1") pin clasp

☐ The hexagonal shape is made in the same way as the dice and houses, first roughly shaped in the fingers, then squared off by tapping against a flat surface. Finish off with a flat piece of wood.

☐ The coil is twisted into the flower shape as it is applied to the pin.

☐ When thoroughly dry, paint and varnish to finish. Glue a pin clasp to the back.

Alternative ideas

Model tiny blocks for original buttons. Model smaller versions of the pins for ear-rings and pendants. Make larger ones to stick on the lids of jars, or use them as repeat motifs to stick on as relief decorations—as tiles around the sink or bathroom, for example.

Steve Bicknell

Make a miniature of your own house— just follow the step-by-step instructions.

Objects for impressing patterns.

Nelson Hargreaves

Combine impressed and relief patterns.

Add a flower in relief for a pin.

Chris Lewis

Clay dice are decorative and useful.

61

Florentine stitched cases

Yarn —
needlepoint 2

Yarn	Length per skein or ball	Canvas size	Needle size
Anchor Tapisserie Wool DMC Laine Tapisserie Appleton's Tapestry Wool Appleton's Crewel Wool (4 strands)	13.7m (15yd) 8m (8yd) 13.7m (15yd) 27.5m (30yd)	14 threads per 2.5cm (1″) single canvas	18
Anchor Tapisserie Wool DMC Laine Tapisserie Appleton's Tapestry Wool Appleton's Crewel Wool (3 strands)	13.7m (15yd) 8m (8yd) 13.7m (15yd) 27.5m (30yd)	16 threads per 2.5cm (1″) single canvas	18
DMC Retors à Broder Coton du Pinguin	10m (11yd) 160m (175yd)	16 threads per 2.5cm (1″) single canvas	18
Appleton's Crewel Wool (2 strands) Clarks Linen Embroidery Anchor Stranded Cotton	27.5m (30yd) 15.5m (17yd) 8m (8yd)	24 threads per 2.5cm (1″) single canvas	22

Florentine embroidery is the name applied to a whole range of needlepoint designs which are worked in straight stitch. Also known as Hungarian Point or Bargello, most forms of Florentine stitch are worked over four or six threads in a variety of patterns, creating strong, geometrical shapes and striking visual effects. As straight stitch does not distort the canvas unduly, you will not need a frame when making small objects.

Although Florentine stitches can be used to create very elaborate and complicated designs, the simplest and two of the most characteristic patterns, zigzag and flame, look impressive but are very straightforward and quick to work. Each row of a separate color is worked horizontally across the canvas, with either a step up or down from stitch to stitch. Once one line of color has been worked, all the others will follow suit. If you have to join the yarn midway across a row, finish off the old thread by threading it through the back of the stitches and begin a new thread in the same way.

Zigzag is the simplest pattern of all. The zigzag base line forms regular peaks, which can be either very deep or fairly shallow. For small objects, a pattern that repeats about every ten stitches is suitable (fig.1). The stitches are usually worked over four threads and back two, which gives a pleasing regular pattern.

Zigzag stitch looks good either in subtly shaded colors, or in vivid, contrasting colors.

Left: 18th-century American silk needlepoint shows the subtle shading of flame stitch. Also used here (section with flowers) is bricking stitch; this is very similar to Florentine but is worked horizontally instead of in a zigzag.

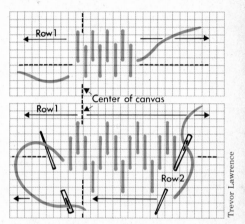

Steve Bicknell

1. *Zigzag stitch, shown from the front (top) and the back (lower row).*

Flame patterns are slightly more complicated, forming steep peaks of varying heights to give a variety of designs. This stitch is usually worked over four threads and back one (fig.2). Flame stitch looks best when worked in a range of toning colors for a subtly shaded effect.

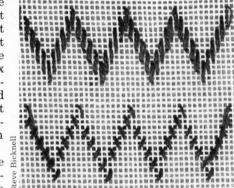

2. *This sample of flame stitch shows how economical the use of yarn is.*

Stitching notes. The easiest way to stitch Florentine is in two movements —put the needle in at the front and take it out from the back, putting it into the next position from the back. Repeat from the front. Working in this way it is easier to see the threads for counting. If you do make a mistake, cut it out rather than rip it—the yarn gets so worn with ripping it is impossible to use it again.

Base line. Most Florentine designs are begun with one row worked right across the width of the design—called the base line, although it is often worked in the center of the canvas to keep the pattern symmetrical. Zigzag and flame can be started with a base line anywhere on the canvas and all other rows will follow automatically above and below.

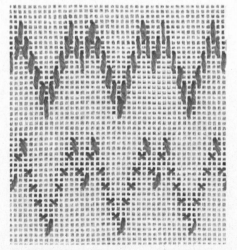

Trevor Lawrence

3. *Above: the base line for bricking stitch, which is a very simplified version of Florentine stitch. Below: the base line for a simple zigzag pattern, showing how to start the second line.*

Pattern repeats. An important aspect of all Florentine designs is to make sure that the base line consists of a complete number of pattern repeats and that each side of the design is symmetrical. Both zigzag and flame stitch build up their patterns from one base line in such a way that they can be started at any point on the canvas. Once the first row has been worked, the others follow almost automatically. The pattern is repeated above and below the base line. Where necessary, work ½-stitches at the edges to fill in the finished square or rectangle.

Estimating yarn length

As zigzag and flame stitch are always worked in horizontal rows, by calculating the amount of yarn needed to work one complete row it then becomes easy to estimate the total amount of yarn required to work a design of a given size. Working with a 46cm (18″) length of yarn, stitch as much of the pattern repeat as this will work. Count the number of lengths needed to fill the row. Multiply again by the number of rows to be worked in each separate color—each stitch covers four horizontal threads, so divide the total number of horizontal threads by four to get the number of complete rows. This gives the total amount of yarn required. The chart shown here gives the lengths of different manufacturers' skeins, so you can work out how many skeins you need.

Varying canvas sizes

A basic stitch like zigzag or flame can easily be translated onto larger or smaller canvas, using the appropriate yarn (see chart).

The base line is worked as before, but the number of pattern repeats will be different if covering the same area on larger or smaller canvas. However, if working a pair of objects, one larger and one small, then the smaller object can be worked on a smaller size canvas with exactly the same design reduced in scale.

To calculate the pattern size on different sizes of canvas, count the number of threads covered by one pattern repeat. For example, in the patterns shown here the zigzag covers 10 threads and flame covers 14.

All canvas is measured by the number of threads per 2.5cm (1"), so divide the number of threads across the width you want to work by the number of threads covered by one pattern repeat. This will give the number of pattern repeats you can work in the base line. Remember to work an exact number of pattern repeats and to keep the base line symmetrical.

Pattern symmetry. If you are making a small object like a glasses case, you can achieve stitch symmetry by counting how many pattern repeats can be worked in the base line, as described above. You can start at one side of the canvas and work in horizontal rows straight across. However, for larger objects like pillows this system is unsuitable because of the number of threads to be counted. So, for larger embroideries which need to be symmetrical, begin stitching at the marked center lines of the canvas. Stitch the first row only from the center outward. Subsequent rows can be stitched straight across the whole width of the design, beginning at the point where the first row ends (fig.3).

Check carefully the number of stitches in the base line. A mistake is hard to spot in the early stages, but will ruin the completed embroidery.

If your base line is accurate there is no need to count stitches again.

Pretty presents to brighten any hand-bag—lighter and glasses case in zigzag stitch, lighter and compact set in flame.

Florentine designs

As an introduction to Florentine stitch these designs are small and manageable and can be made up in no time at all. Yet they show off well the characteristically subtle shading of Florentine embroidery. This stitch shows results quickly and you can produce a great variety of beautiful and practical objects—excellent for gifts. In the designs shown here the glasses case and the compact case are worked on a medium canvas, while the two lighter cases show exactly the same designs scaled down on a fine canvas.

All these designs make excellent ways of using up scraps of yarn left over from other projects.

Zigzag specs case

Completed size: 15cm x 6.5cm (6"x2½")
You will need:
Canvas 16 threads per 2.5cm (1"), measuring 20cm x 13cm (8"x5").
Yarn (see chart) 24 pieces each 46cm (18") long. Shown here are 7 shades of browns and beiges — 3 pieces each of 4 shades and 4 pieces of the other 3 shades.
Lining fabric, 17.5cm x 9cm (7"x3½")
For back of case, 15cm x 6.5cm (6"x2½") of suede, leather or felt
Matching sewing thread and needle
☐ Mark the center of the canvas horizontally and vertically and mark in the dimensions of the specs case. Either fold masking tape over the edges of the canvas, or overcast with yarn. Trim away when making up.
☐ Following the diagram for zigzag stitch (fig.4), work one horizontal base

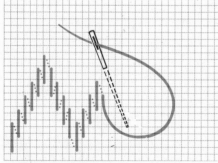

4. *Zigzag stitch detail.*

line anywhere across the narrow canvas width. This will comprise 4 zigzag pattern repeats and will use one 46cm (18") length of yarn.
☐ Using a different color yarn for each row, build up the pattern in toning shades of brown.
To make up. Pin the canvas to shape on an ironing board and press under a damp cloth. Leave to dry thoroughly. Trim the canvas to within 1.5cm (½") of the worked area. Trim the lining fabric to the same size. Fold the canvas seam allowance to the back of the work, mitering the corners. Herring-

bone to the back of the embroidery (fig.5).

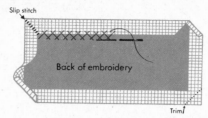

5. *Miter corners and herringbone canvas to back of embroidery.*

☐ Turn under the lining fabric seam allowance and miter the corners in the same way as the canvas. Slip stitch the lining to the back of the embroidery, wrong sides facing.
☐ Cut the back of the case to the completed size of the case and overcast neatly to the canvas around 3 sides.

Zigzag lighter case

Completed size: 7.5cm x 4.5cm (3"x1¾")
You will need:
Canvas, 24 threads per 2.5cm (1"), measuring 13cm x 10cm (5"x4").
Yarn (see chart) 19 pieces each 30cm (12") long. Shown here are 7 shades of browns, beiges and pinks — 3 pieces each of 5 colors, 2 pieces of 2 colors.
Lining fabric, 10cm x 7cm (4"x2¾")
For back of case, 7.5cm x 4.5cm (3"x1¾") of suede, leather or felt
Matching sewing thread and needle
☐ Mark the center of the canvas horizontally and vertically and mark in the dimensions of the lighter case. Either fold masking tape over the edges of the canvas, or overcast with yarn. Trim away when making up.
☐ Following the diagram for zigzag stitch (fig.4), work one horizontal base line anywhere across the narrow canvas width. This will comprise 4 zigzag pattern repeats.
☐ Continue to build up the pattern in rows of different colored yarns.
☐ Make up the lighter case in the same way as for the glasses case above.

Flame compact case

Completed size: 9.5cm x 9.5cm (3¾"x3¾")
You will need:
Canvas, 16 threads per 2.5cm (1"), measuring 14cm x 14cm (5½"x5½").
Yarn (see chart) 16 pieces each 46cm (18") long. Shown here are 6 shades of pink — 3 pieces each of 5 shades and one strand of the sixth shade.
Lining fabric, 12cm x 12cm (4¾"x4¾")
For back of case 9.5cm x 9.5cm (3¾"x3¾") of suede, leather or felt
Matching sewing thread and needle 46cm (½yd) matching cord or braid (you can make handmade cords by braiding together one or more of the yarns used in the embroidery)
☐ Mark the center of the canvas horizontally and vertically and mark in

the dimensions of the compact case. Either fold masking tape over the edges of the canvas, or overcast with yarn. Trim away when making up.
☐ Following the diagram for flame stitch (fig.6), work one horizontal base

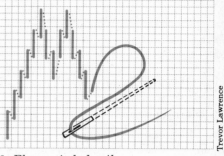

6. *Flame stitch detail.*

line anywhere within the marked outline. This will comprise 4 pattern repeats.
☐ Using a different shade of yarn for each row, build up the pattern in toning shades of pink.
☐ Make up the compact case in the same way as for the glasses case above but, when attaching the back, leave 6mm (¼") open at one lower corner.
☐ Slip stitch the cord all around the edge of the canvas. Tuck in the ends and close the opening neatly.

Flame lighter case

Completed size: 6.5cm x 6.5cm (2½"x 2½")
You will need:
Canvas 24 threads per 2.5cm (1"), measuring 11.5cm x 11.5cm (4½"x4½").
Yarn (see chart) 15 pieces each 30cm (12") long. Shown here are 5 shades of pinks and beiges — 3 pieces of each shade.
Lining fabric, 9cm x 9cm (3½"x3½")
For back of case 6.5cm x 6.5cm (2½"x2½") of suede, leather or felt
30cm (12") matching cord or braid (bought or handmade from yarn braided by hand)
☐ Mark the center of the canvas horizontally and vertically and mark in the dimensions of the lighter case. Either fold masking tape over the edges of the canvas, or overcast with yarn. Trim away when making up.
☐ Following the diagram for flame stitch (fig.6), work one horizontal base line anywhere within the marked outline. This will comprise 4 pattern repeats.
☐ Using a different shade of yarn for each row, build up the pattern in toning shades.
☐ Make up in the same way as for the glasses case above but, when attaching the back, leave 6mm (¼") open at the lower corner.
☐ Slip stitch the cord all around the edge of the canvas. Tuck in the ends and close the opening neatly.

Finger weaving peasant braids

Weaving terms
Warp—a set of vertical yarns through which the weft is passed when forming a fabric.
Warp end—each warp length is called an end.
Weft—the yarn that is passed through the warp ends in a horizontal direction.

Finger weaving is a process of making woven cloth by using your fingers to guide the wefts through the warp ends. As well as being the simplest form of weaving it is also thought to be the oldest. Examples of ancient braids woven by this method have been found in almost every part of the world. People in places as far apart as Peru, Egypt and Scandinavia worked out patterns by manipulating various colors of yarn with their fingers.

Finger weaving travels well! Because you need no tools, it is the ideal pastime while traveling or sitting in the garden or on the beach.

The easiest patterns to make in finger weaving are diagonal bands of color.

From this basic method wavy lines of color can be woven as illustrated. Once the principle of separating the warp ends and inserting the wefts has been achieved, chevron and diamond patterns can be worked by grouping the yarn differently and weaving it in two directions. And so the progression, towards the complex grouping of yarns to produce double woven braids, is easy.

Uses for bands of finger weaving

Use the braids for decorating sweaters and woolen dresses, for making into belts, book marks, cuffs, napkin rings, watchstraps, chokers, bracelets, hatbands and sashes.

Braid widths

Although finger weaving is primarily useful for weaving narrow bands using about 16 strands, wider pieces can be made—with practice. The maximum number of strands which can be handled comfortably is about 48, however the width of the finished braid will depend on the thickness of the yarn. Narrow bands may be sewn together to make either wide bands of color, wall hangings, place mats, pillows, totes, shoulder- or handbags. Braids can also be joined by working several braids simultaneously and intertwining the outside strands of each set.

Materials

The materials needed for finger weaving are simple and inexpensive. All you need is yarn—rug wool, knitting wool or cotton or synthetic yarn—and a pencil to which to attach the yarn. Use sports yarn to begin with as this is the simplest to use. After learning the skill of finger weaving, interesting effects can be produced by using heavy wools and string or fine silks and cottons.

Color

Color is fundamental to weaving and the choice of color combinations should be given some thought before a project is started. When choosing color schemes for braids to decorate clothes, choose one color which picks up or matches the color of the garment. Experiment with colors and combinations of color because the play of color can be one of the most exciting parts of your work.

Finger weaving relies heavily on the use of color contrasts. Strong contrasts produce a bold effect and accentuate the pattern, while subtle combinations create a softer mood and give a more subtle pattern which can be equally effective. Alternatively, use a small amount of a neutral color to 'break up' bands of primary colors. Sections of 3 or 4 colors containing 6, 7 or 8 strands give an effective result although more or less can be used.

To make a belt or anything else which needs to have a fringe at each end, set up as follows:

An assortment of colorful braids.

Bright hatband which is easy to make.

Preparation

Cutting the yarn. Cut the various colored yarns into the required number of lengths. Each length of yarn should be two or three times as long as the finished length of the article, depending on how long you wish the fringe to be. If you wish to hem the ends, then twice the length is ample. For example, if you are weaving something 15cm (6″) long, cut the yarn 30cm (12″) long. The width of the finished braid will be about ½-¾ of the width of the yarn wound around the pencil and squeezed together.

First of all anchor the yarn firmly to some immovable object by tying an overhand knot at one end of the bunch of yarns and looping over a hook, door knob, chair or drawer handle (fig.1), or by pinning them securely to a cork board.

1. *Loop yarn over an immovable object.*

Wind each strand in turn around a pencil, about 5cm (2″) below the knot, (fig.2).

2. *Winding strands around pencil.*

Weaving

Set the strands onto the pencil in groups of color, arranging them side by side. Hold the strands toward you about 8cm (3″) below the pencil in the right hand. (These lengths of yarn are called the warp ends.) As the threads are used, pass them to your left hand and hold taut.

☐ Working from left to right, pick up strand A and weave it under strand B, over strand C, under strand D and so on across all the strands (fig.3).

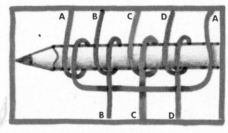

3. *Weave A from left to right.*

☐ Pull strand A parallel to the pencil and, using the forefinger of the left hand, push it up close to the pencil. Tuck strand A over the right end of the pencil.
☐ Pick up strand B and weave it under strand C, over strand D, under the next and so on across all the strands. (You may find it easier to think of the weaving movement as plaiting the traveling strand across.) (fig.4).
☐ Pull strand B parallel to the pencil and push it against the pencil. Remember to push up the strands after they have been carried through the warp ends. The pattern and tension can then be checked for evenness and corrected before the pattern has progressed too far.
To make a selvage on the right hand side, bring strand A either under or over strand B (whichever completes the weaving sequence) and place it parallel to the other warp ends. Tuck strand B over the pencil. The method of making the selvage is the same for whatever pattern you are weaving (fig.5).

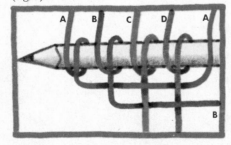

4. *Weave B from left to right.*

☐ Pick up strand C and weave it under the second warp end, over the third, under the fourth and so on across the warp ends.
☐ Continue weaving each warp end on

the far left, using it as a weft, through the warp ends, always reversing the sequence of the previous row and bringing every weft down over or under the lower one to complete the selvage on the right hand side (fig.5).

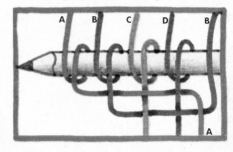

5. *Bring A over B to make a selvage.*

Make sure the strands aren't getting tangled—sort them out as you go along. Pull each horizontal strand firmly but not too tightly and give the warp ends a gentle straightening pull after each movement. The horizontal strands should be completely covered by the warp ends.

For the first 5 or 10 minutes it will probably seem like an awful lot of strands and nothing effective happening. Then suddenly you begin to build up rhythm to achieve an even tension and the diagonal pattern starts to grow under your fingers. From that moment on you'll be hooked!

Make sure that you pull the right selvage firmly, in a straight line. Otherwise the band will begin to curve. (Of course, you can turn this into a virtue when you are making a collar or a hatband.)

If you want a fringe at the end of the braid leave 20cm-25cm (8″-10″) of warp ends for finishing.

Diagonal stripes

For diagonal stripes, set the threads in groups. The 3-color sample below has 8 orange, 8 pink and 8 yellow. Follow the weaving process, working always from left to right.

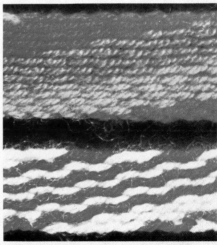

Three- and two-color diagonal stripes.

Numerals on diagrams indicate number of strands needed to give patterns shown on left.

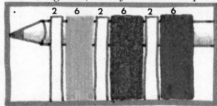

Red and white diagonal stripes.

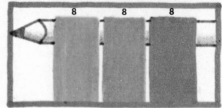

Wide diagonal, candy-colored stripes.

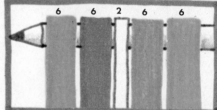

Wavy lines with single strands of white.

A wavy line on a yellow background.

Chevron pattern in four colors.

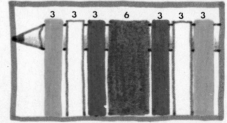

Alternating chevron pattern.

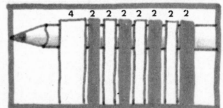

Chevrons make diamond patterns too.

Wavy line stripes

Arrange the strands as for diagonal stripes and follow the weaving process. The same method is followed as given for diagonal stripes, until all the warp ends have been used once as a weft.

☐ Then complete the selvage on the right hand side and, with the last weft that you used, weave it in and out of the warp ends from right to left.

☐ Pick up the far right warp end and weave it in and out, working from right to left also.

☐ To make the selvage on the left hand side, bring the upper weft either under or over the lower weft (whichever completes the sequence) and place it parallel to the warp ends.

☐ Continue in this way, working from right to left, until you want the bands of color to curve in the reverse direction. If you wish, the change in direction may be made at any point, but the largest curves are achieved by using all the warp ends as wefts before changing direction.

Chevron pattern

Choose an even number of colors and strands. Divide each pile into two groups, with the same sequence of colors, and mount them on a pencil so that when the warp ends are divided in the middle the color sequence of one group is reflected exactly in the other group (see opposite).

☐ Grip the left group of warp ends in your left hand and the right group in your right hand.

☐ Then, using the forefinger and thumb of your right hand, pick up the first warp end at the right edge of the left group.

☐ Weave this warp end (which is now the weft) over, under, over the warp ends in the right hand.

☐ Pull the weft parallel to the pencil. Grasp all the warp ends in the right group in your right hand except the one on the far left of this group.

☐ Pass this warp end (now the weft) over, under, over, working from right to left through the warp ends held in the left hand.

☐ Return to the right group of warp ends and pass the far right warp end from the left group over, under, over the warp ends held in the right hand.

☐ Repeat this movement with the left group, by passing the far left warp end from the right group over, under, over through the left group of warp ends.

☐ Form a selvage on the right and left sides (fig.5) as you go.

☐ Continue weaving from the center to the edges until the color you started with on the far left and far right is positioned in the center of the warp ends. You have now worked one chevron pattern. Continue in this way until you have worked the required length.

Chevron pattern with diamond shape

☐ Mount the strands of yarn on a pencil by tying them halfway along their length in the same sequence as for chevron pattern, (see opposite).

☐ Tie one lot of warp ends in a loose knot—to keep them out of the way while you are weaving the others.

☐ Using the free strands, work the required length in the chevron pattern. Untie the loose knot and the knots around the pencil. Turn the work around, but not over, so the unworked ends are toward you and weave chevron patterns as before. Because you are working in the opposite direction, a diamond shape is formed in the center.

Finishing

A neat finish enhances any braid, so either knot, turn under and neatly hem or finish in one of the following ways to give a 'fringe' effect.

Even if you want a simple fringe, it will lie better if you start with a small amount of braiding or ply before knotting. Knots straight after finger weaving tend to splay and look untidy.

Braids. If the number of warp ends are multiples of three, braid sets of three warp ends. Knot the ends and trim them level or at an angle.

With a little practice even numbers of warps, if they are multiples of four, may be braided using four strands.

Ply. Take a pair of warp ends. Twist one warp end between your thumb and forefinger to the right until it is very tightly twisted and begins to kink even when held fairly taut. Secure the end with a pin to a cushion or stick it to a table with sticky tape so that it can't unwind. Repeat the twisting with the other warp end and hold it firmly. Pick up the first twisted warp end and hold it firmly too. Hold both warp ends together between your thumb and forefinger and tug firmly while rolling the warp ends toward the left. Release the warp ends. They

Finishes: ply, plait and small knot.

should twist together, that is, form a ply. Knot the ends and trim them. Repeat with the remaining warp ends.

Knots. Finish braids and ply by tying knots across the bottom of the sets of braided and plied strands. To make a small knot, take only one of the

strands, wrap it round 2 strands, make a single knot and pull tight. Trim the strands either just below the knots, or leave a little tassel.

Hems. Tie strands in pairs with a double knot and trim ends as close as possible to the knots without weakening them. Turn the knotted ends in 6mm (¼″) to the wrong side and fold again 2cm (¾″) from the edge. Using the same colored yarn, make neat stab stitches through the braid to prevent the ends from unfolding.

Decorative choker in diamond pattern.

To make the choker

The choker shown is about 2cm (¾″) wide and 38cm (15″) long, including 5cm (2″) for finishing. Adjust the length according to your requirements by working a little more or a little less.

☐ Choose yarn in four colors and cut into 76cm (30″) lengths, in the quantities given in the diagram at the bottom of the opposite page.

☐ Mount the center of each length of yarn on a pencil in the sequence indicated and tie the warp ends that you are not working with in a loose knot. Work 19cm (7½″) in a chevron pattern. Untie the loose knot and the knots around the pencil. Turn the unworked warp ends around, but not over, and continue with the chevron pattern until the length is 38cm (15″).

☐ Arrange warp ends at each end of the band in pairs and knot them. This prevents the work from unraveling.

☐ Turn each knotted end of the band 6mm (¼″) to the wrong side. Turn each end 2cm (¾″) under again and stitch the folded edges to the wrong side.

☐ Make a fastening by sewing a 12mm (½″) button to the right side of the band near one edge. Make a loop at the other edge by passing a 10cm (4″) strand of yarn through the folded hem. Knot the two ends together, adjusting to the right length. Trim the ends and thread the knot inside the hem so that it is hidden. The loop will then fasten over the button and secure the band.

Make a warm padded quilt

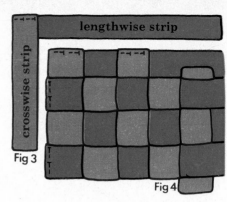

Fig 3 crosswise strip / lengthwise strip

Fig 4

Making a conventional quilt on an ordinary sewing machine is often impossible because there's a limit to the amount of bulk you can feed through. This woven quilt does not involve stitching through batting and is simply made up from lots of separate tubes, filled with strips of batting and woven together to give a luxuriously padded quilt.

Choose two color schemes of the same print to accentuate the texture of the unusual giant-size weave, or use remnants of several different fabrics to create a patchwork effect. You need a minimum of 45cm (½yd) for each crosswise tube and 1.8m (2yd) for each lengthwise tube.

Twin bed quilt

For a quilt 87cm x 177cm (35"x71")
You will need: Using 90cm (36") wide fabric (dress cotton)
For crosswise tubes (red), 4.25m (4½yd)

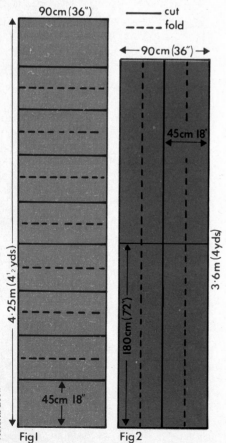

90cm (36") — cut / --- fold

90cm (36")

45cm 18"

4.25m (4½ yds)

180cm (72")

3.6m (4yds)

45cm 18"

Fig1   **Fig2**

Victoria Drew

For lengthwise tubes (blue), 3.6m (4yd)
95cm (38") wide Fortrel or Dacron batting, 4m (4¾yd)
Matching sewing thread
Long glass-headed pins

To make 9 crosswise (red) tubes. Following the cutting layout (fig.1) cut the 4.25m (4½yd) length of fabric into 9 strips each 90cm x 45cm (36"x18").

☐ With right sides facing, fold each 45cm (18") wide strip in half along the length and stitch down long sides, taking a 1.5cm (½") seam allowance which is given throughout. Be sure to fold strips along straight of grain.

☐ You now have 9 tubes 90cm (36") long and 21cm (8½") wide. Press the seams open and, with the seam along one side, close one end of each tube by machine. Turn the tubes to the right side and press again.

To make 4 lengthwise (blue) tubes. Following the cutting layout (fig.2) cut the fabric into 2 equal lengths and cut each piece in half lengthwise to give 4 strips 180cm (72") by 45cm (18").

Fold along the length and make up as crosswise (red) tubes.

Making up the quilt. Cut a length of batting 180cm x 95cm (72"x 38"). Cut this into 4 strips 180cm x 23cm (72"x9½"). Cut the remaining batting into 9 strips 90cm x 23cm (36"x9½").

☐ Insert a length of batting into each tube, feeding it in carefully so as not to pull it apart. Turn in the raw edges of each tube and close either with slip stitching or machine. If stitching, stitch very close to the edge to give a neat finish.

Weaving together involves assembling the quilt on the floor, so start by marking out a right angle.

☐ First lay a lengthwise (blue) tube and then a crosswise (red) tube on top of it, following the lines of the right angle.

☐ Pin down the ends of each tube securely using long glass-headed pins (fig.3).

☐ Line up the other 3 lengthwise tubes side by side, going over and under the crosswise strip alternately. Pin down in position.

☐ Take each remaining crosswise tube and weave it in and out of the long tubes, overlapping the edges very slightly so no gaps appear (fig.4).

Secure at each end to a lengthwise tube.

☐ To complete, overcast (oversew) tubes together all around the outside.

Double bed quilt

For a quilt 177cm x 177cm (71"x71")
You will need: Using 90cm (36") wide fabric (dress cotton)
For crosswise tubes, 9m (10yd)
For lengthwise tubes, 7.2m (8yd)
95cm (38") wide Fortrel or Dacron batting, 9m (10yd)

Cutting 9 crosswise tubes. Cut the fabric into five 180cm (2yd) lengths and cut each piece lengthwise to give 9 strips 45cm x 180cm (18"x72").

Cutting 8 lengthwise tubes. Cut the fabric into four 180cm (2yd) lengths and cut each piece lengthwise to make 8 strips 45cm x 180cm (18"x72").

Making up. Cut the batting into 17 strips each 180cm x 23cm (72"x9½"). Make up into tubes, fill and weave together as twin bed quilts.

Basic sewing Know-how

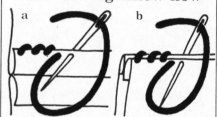

a   b

Overcasting: *usually worked from left to right. It is a good stitch for finishing off raw seam edges by hand (a). Overcasting also provides a strong stitch for joining two folded edges together (b).*

Slip stitch: *worked from right to left to give an invisible finish and used here to sew two folded edges together invisibly.*

Jerry Tubby

Applying a finish to wood

All woodwork needs finishing. When it has lost the natural protection of its coat of bark, the timber inside, however attractive it looks in its raw state, will soon lose its appeal and become warped and dirty. As well as looking un- attractive, this will harm the wood and shorten its life.

Craftsmen of old spent years learning to create and apply delicate finishes, such as French polish. Nowadays, however, there is a wide choice of finishes which are easy to apply. These range from virtually transparent ones, which will complement and preserve the wood without changing its ap- pearance much, to finishes that will darken the wood or add a bright, modern color, which will nonetheless let the grain show through.

Modern finishes have largely super- seded many older and more fragile ones, such as French or Button polish and varnishes based on shellac or cellulose. French polish is still used occasionally on new work because it gives a superb, mirror-like finish. But it needs skillful application and should be left to an expert. French polish also has very little resistance to heat or water, while polyurethanes, which give almost as good a finish, are easier to apply and much more hardwearing. There are several modern commercial substitutes for French polish which are less difficult to apply and rather more resistant to water and alcohol. But these still need very careful application and have almost no resistance to heat.

Wax polish

This is one of the easiest finishes to apply and produces a lovely soft sheen, with a slightly yellowish tinge. But it does show up fingerprints and other marks and has very little resistance to heat. It is best used, therefore, on decorative surfaces or on any piece that is not likely to be handled.

Wax polish was originally based on beeswax, often in combination with carnauba wax, which is derived from the leaves of a plant found in Brazil. Wax polish is obtainable in a large number of commercial brands or you can make it yourself (see below). The commercial brands will usually have silicone ingredients and additives to

Pine

Oak

Walnut

Teak

Red Mahogany

Dark oak
Polyurethane finishes in wood tones, shown on whitewood.

Steve Bicknell

improve their protective qualities or to add a pleasant smell.

One of the best ways of finishing raw wood is to seal it with one or two coats of clear polyurethane and then wax on top, although you can wax without pre-sealing. Apply the wax with a cloth, sparingly, and then buff it up with a clean cloth or a very soft brush. Re-coat with wax and buff up again. Repeat this process, allowing a day or two in between for the wax to harden, until you have a good, deep gloss. Rubbing down with very fine (000 or 0000 grade) steel wool gives a smooth, hardwearing but less glossy surface.

To make beeswax polish
You will need:
Beeswax
Turpentine

☐ Shred beeswax into a vessel standing in hot water. Add barely enough tur- pentine to cover it and stir thoroughly until a paste is formed.

You can do this without standing the vessel in hot water; it will just take a little longer to break down the bees- wax. Do *not* allow a naked flame near the mixture, since turpentine is highly inflammable and so is its vapor. *Never* warm it over a stove.

☐ You can use powdered earth colors, obtainable from suppliers of artists' materials, or lamp black to color the polish. If you experiment like this, do try it on a piece of scrap wood or an inconspicuous area first—this is always a good idea when handling a process you have not tried before.

☐ Stir the paste well and store it in an airtight container.

Linseed oil

This gives a good, traditional finish which improves with age and repeated applications. It darkens the wood and tends to collect dirt and rub off on clothing in its early days. It is most suitable for dark woods such as teak, but should not be used on food con- tainers since it is liable to leave a taste on food.

Linseed oil is obtainable at any hard- ware store, under many brand names. It can be bought boiled or raw. The boiled form (which has, in fact, been heated carefully until it thickens, rather than boiled) is preferable, as it dries quicker, having been partially oxidized before application.

The oil is applied by rubbing in with a rag. If you want to minimize discolora- tion, dilute the linseed oil with an equal part of turpentine. Use it sparingly, rub on a very thin coat and leave it for a couple of hours. There should be no surplus; if there is some, wipe it off. Let the wood dry thoroughly before applying any more oil.

Repeat the operation every day for two

Shelves made from whitewood (see Carpentry, chapter 2) can be finished in the color of a darker wood.

or three weeks, until the wood will accept no more. Rub hard with a soft cloth to bring up the finish. You may use a final coat of wax polish to improve the shine.

Teak oil

A modern alternative to linseed oil is teak oil, which is quicker-drying and tends to color the wood rather more. It is, as its name suggests, best on teak but it is suitable for any dark, coarse-textured hardwood. It can be used on softwoods but these usually benefit from a tougher finish.

Teak oil is applied in the same way as linseed oil.

Vegetable oil

You can use olive oil to finish salad bowls or any wooden food container. Any corn oil, as sold for cooking, will also do. Rub it in with a rag, as for linseed oil. The finish will be a soft sheen rather than a high polish.

Polyurethane wood finishes

These are the results of modern technological developments which have produced an extremely tough, translucent finish. It can be obtained either clear or in a wide range of colors

Chris Lewis

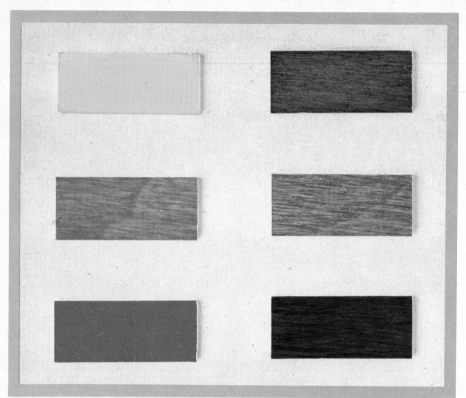

from natural wood shades to bright reds and greens. Whatever color you use, it will not obscure the grain of the wood, which can be seen through the finish. The clear varieties, which, like all finishes, give some discoloration, are available in both matt and gloss, or these can be mixed for an intermediate effect.

The principal advantage of polyurethanes is their durability—they will withstand almost any damage once they have set, even boiling water; though heat, transmitted through a polyurethaned surface, may eventually damage the wood underneath. You must, however, take care when applying them, especially as some varieties may take two weeks to achieve maximum hardness.

The water-resistant properties of polyurethanes make them especially suitable for kitchens and bathrooms, but they can be used anywhere.

Commercial brands are available at any hardware store, in either one- or two-pack varieties. It is most important to follow the manufacturer's instructions, especially for the two-pack varieties which have to be mixed before application. These are generally quicker-drying but you must be careful to get the proportions right (these vary between makes) and not to mix too much, since the mixture will not keep longer than a day. The one-pack types can be used straight from the can, which should be re-closed tightly after use.

Polyurethane finishes should be applied directly to the sanded wood, which must be clean and dry. Avoid working in humid atmospheres. For best results, dilute the first coat with an equal amount of thinner, to help it soak in and seal the wood, and apply it with a cloth pad. When the first coat is dry, sand it down lightly before applying another. Subsequent coats may be diluted in the proportion of one part thinner to three parts polyurethane to give thinner coats which will brush on more easily.

For a clear finish, two coats may be sufficient; if you anticipate very hard wear, then use more. The thicker the coats you use, the tougher the finish will be—but a thinner finish will look more attractive.

Colored polyurethanes can be used to add interest to pine or other light-wood furniture. You can either use the color of a darker wood or a

Polyurethane wood finishes are available in a wide variety of colors, as shown in the samples (above left). The exact shade of the finish will depend on the color of the wood and the number of coats used. By mixing different colors and varying the number of coats, you can achieve different shades.

Steve Bicknell

bright, modern color. Whichever you choose, the grain will still be visible: the more pronounced the grain of the wood, the better the effect is likely to be. Beware of using the brighter colors on dark wood, as the color of the wood will affect them. The color will also deepen with repeated coats.

Before applying colored polyurethane it is advisable to seal the wood with a coat of clear polyurethane, bought from the same manufacturer to ensure compatability. This will forestall any problems arising from varying absorbency of the wood, which could cause a patchy result if the colored

The use of colored finishes can add interest to inexpensive furniture.

finish is absorbed in different amounts. Thereafter, apply in the same way as clear polyurethane. If you want a matt finish, a final coat of clear, matt polyurethane is the answer.

Vegetable and fruit blocking

Color — printing 1

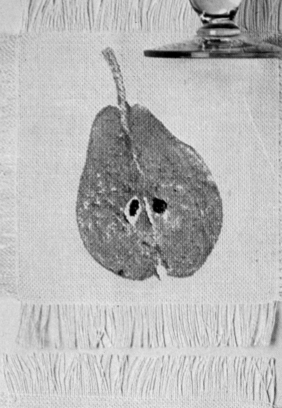

Relief printing using fruit and vegetables is a basic printing technique, making use of the intrinsic designs of nature and simple printing procedures. Try your hand at relief printing with these glass mats which, together with the shopping bag overleaf, were designed by Janet Allen.

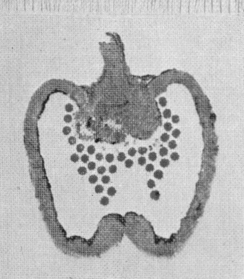

To put it at its simplest, relief printing usually involves applying color to one surface and pressing the color onto another surface. You can print onto all sorts of surfaces including paper, cloth and walls: the type of paint or ink you choose will depend on what you are printing.

Most relief printing methods involve the making of a printing block, but there are some objects—such as fruits—which in themselves are ready-made printing blocks.

Numerous fruits and vegetables have attractive shapes and inherent patterns. If, for example, you cut horizontally across an onion you reveal an eminently printable pattern of rings. Cut it vertically and you have another kind of pattern. The fruits or vegetables need to be fairly hard and firm—a tomato, for instance, is far too squashy—but apples, pears, cabbages, leeks and celery are a few of the suitable types.

Paints, inks and dyes

Water-solvent paints. For relief printing poster paint or powder colors should be of a thick consistency. Block printing watercolors may be used undiluted. You only require water for cleaning up afterward. The color can be applied with a stiff brush or you can use a sponge pad which is impregnated with color and used as a stamping pad. These paints are not washable and are therefore really only suitable for paper. Paper printed with water-solvent color may be varnished (when the print is absolutely dry) with paper varnish. This prolongs its life and makes it waterproof.

Oil-bound printing ink and fabric printing colors work best on fruit and vegetables if diluted with a very little paint thinner. These inks are waterproof and fabric printing colors are washable. They require turpentine for cleaning up afterward.

Fabric printing dyes are suitable for large, broad shapes but are slightly too liquid to pick up intricate patterns with this kind of printing. These dyes are washable and can be fixed by ironing the fabric. Use a temperature suitable for the type of fabric. Manufacturers give details of fixing procedures for their particular dyes.

Papers and fabrics

Do not use a non-absorbent, glossy paper because your printing object will tend to slide when you press it down. Newsprint is ideal for trial prints but it is inclined to become yellow within a short time and is easily torn. After first experimenting on cheap newsprint or newspaper, use a cartridge type of paper. Colored papers can add interest to the design.

This method of relief printing requires the minimum of equipment.

Melvin Grey

The fabric printing colors and dyes work best on natural fiber fabrics. Some man-made fiber fabrics are not fast to washing or cleaning when printed. If in doubt, test a piece of printed fabric first. Cloth which is heavily starched when new should be washed and ironed before printing.

Preparing the fruit and vegetables

Have ready plenty of table space, a chopping board, a selection of sharp kitchen knives and some rags.

Experiment by cutting your fruits and vegetables in half, into quarters, diagonally across and at different points. Do not remove any peel or skin as it both defines the shape and helps to hold the cut piece together.

Most fruits and vegetables are rather wet when cut so it is advisable to dry them first gently with a rag.

To make the glass mats

You will need:

Firm pear and apple and a green pepper, all with good, clear shapes
Sharp knife
Fabric printing dyes
Stiff brush (eg small house-painting brush); small artist's paintbrush
Suitable fabric such as linen (enough for 4 squares, allowing an extra 5cm (2″) all around each one)
Scraps of fabric for trial prints
Rags and old blanket or piece of felt
Needle and thread

☐ Determine how large you want the mats to be and cut the linen into squares 5cm (2″) larger all round than final size—you will trim them down after printing. This makes it easier to center the motif accurately. The mats shown here are 15cm (6″) square, including a 2cm (¾″) fringe.

☐ Place a piece of felt or blanket on a table to give some softness underneath the fabric being printed. Place your fabric on top of this.

☐ Slice the fruit or vegetable in half and carefully dry the cut surface.

☐ Apply the dye fairly liberally with the stiff brush and do a test print first on a scrap of fabric.

You may want to apply more than one color, as shown on the apple prints. To do this, simply apply your chosen colors next to each other and gently blend the edges where they meet, using light, even strokes. The colors will merge into each other and you will ob-

Steve Bicknell

tain the best results if you use colors which, when mixed, produce an intermediate color which suits your print. For instance, on one of the apple prints red merges into orange via a reddish-orange. On the other apple print orange merges through yellow to green; both the mixture of orange and yellow and that of yellow and green produce acceptable intermediate colors. If you apply orange immediately next to green, the area where they mix will become brown and rather dark.

You can experiment with blending color with dyes on paper. You may become interested in the whole fascinating subject of color theory. If so, your local library should be able to provide some useful reading on the subject.

When printing, do not bang the fruit down as it may slide around, but carefully place it and apply gentle, even pressure. Some parts such as stalks will need to be pressed down with the end of a pencil. Lift the fruit away from the fabric very carefully.

☐ When you are confident of how much dye to apply and how hard to press to get an even print, go on to make your final prints.

☐ Paint the seeds in afterwards with a paintbrush or, as with the green pepper, with the end of a matchstick.

☐ When the prints are completely dry, iron the fabric to fix the dye.

☐ With a pencil dot at each corner mark the size of square required, excluding the fringe (11cm (4½″) square in the mats illustrated). You may find it

Eyecatching shopping bag—printed with halved fruits or vegetables—makes plain denim look really special.

easier to cut a square of cardboard to the size required: slide it under the fabric and center your motif. Mark each corner of the square with a dot.

☐ Machine stitch from dot to dot, outlining the inner square.

☐ Mark another square, 2cm (¾″) larger all around, and cut the mats to this size.

☐ Now fray the cloth from the cut edge to the line of stitching to make a fringe all around.

To make a shopping bag
You will need:

53cm (21″) of 90cm (36″) wide denim,

linen, heavy muslin or other similar light-colored material.

☐ Cut a piece of fabric 90cm x 45cm (36"x18") for the body of the bag and reserve the strip left over for the handles.

The selvages or 45cm (18") edges form the top edges of the bag.

☐ To find the position for the base of the pears, measure 38cm (15") down from one top edge at each side and mark with a pin. As a guide line pin a strip of paper from side to side at position of pins, to mark the base line of the pears. There is no need for a pencil line which might be difficult to erase later. Print the pears as described for the glass mats.

☐ Mark a 10cm (4") turning along each top edge with a line of running stitches. Take the long strip of fabric and fold in half lengthwise, right sides together. Stitch down long edge, turn right side out and press. Topstitch along sides about 6mm (¼") in from the edge. Cut the strip in half.

☐ Stitch handles to bag as shown, turning raw ends under (fig.1).

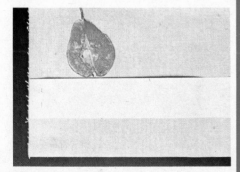

Work topstitching around edges of bag.

☐ Turn under top edges of bag along marked line. Pin in place and press along fold edge.

☐ Work lines of topstitching along the top of the bag edges close to the fold, and down the sides 2.5cm (1") in from the edge.

☐ Fold the bag in half, right sides together, and stitch sides closed taking a 12mm (½") seam allowance. Press seams open and turn right sides out.

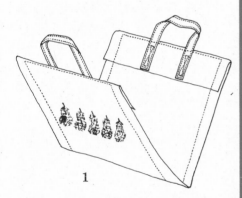

Positioning prints with paper strip.

You can quite simply obtain beautiful printed patterns from most fruit and vegetables. Look closely at those you use everyday and, as you cut them up, think of how they would print and the way color could be used to heighten the effect. The diagram below shows the various cuts and their respective printed effects, all from one leek. Try an onion cut across the middle or even walnut shells or mushrooms.

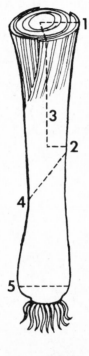

Cut 3: lengthwise

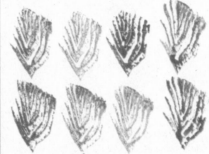

Cut 1: the tips of the leaves

Cut 4: on the diagonal

Cut 5: across the base

Cut 2: across the middle

Cut 5 printed side-by-side

Door curtain from jump rings

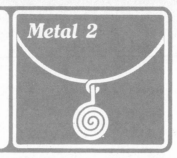

Jump rings can be used in dozens of ways. As shown in Metal Chapter 1, they provide the simplest way to join various sections of jewelry. But they can also be used to join other materials, such as squares of sheet acetate, sheet vinyl, linoleum or foil-covered cardboard, to make decorative hangings.

Making a door curtain

This attractive door curtain is ideal to keep a room cool in hot weather and to keep flies and insects out. It can hang from any door as a room divider and is especially useful if you have limited space and don't want a door closed all the time—you could even remove the door itself. It is also useful hanging between the kitchen and the pantry or to camouflage a long passage in a hall. The door curtain is both inexpensive and easy to make and a good way of using up a spare piece of sheet vinyl flooring or linoleum. Simply cut the flooring into strips and join them together with a series of jump rings. You could improvise by substituting curtain rings for the jump rings.

The lengths given easily cover an average door, but the exact amount of floor covering needed will depend on the size you want to cut the strips and the spacing between the rows. Make the last piece of each strip slightly longer, so that when you hang the strips you can adjust the length by cutting off the excess.

The size of the jump rings will also affect the size of the curtain, as will the position of the holes through which you slip the jump rings. These holes should not be less than 5mm ($\frac{1}{4}''$) from the edge of the rectangles.

You will need:

1.25sq m ($1\frac{1}{2}$sq yd) sheet vinyl flooring or linoleum

37m (40yd) tinned copper wire 1.6mm diameter (14 gauge).

One dowel, 12mm-15mm ($\frac{1}{2}''$-$\frac{3}{4}''$) diameter, long enough to fit the doorway

Tools. Hammer, pair of wire cutters, pliers. For vinyl flooring, heavy scissors and leather punch. For linoleum, utility knife, and bradawl or large nail

□ From the linoleum cut strips 12.5cm x 2.5cm (5"x1"). Cut vinyl floor covering with scissors, linoleum with utility knife. For an average door you will need 392 pieces to make 28 strips each with 14 pieces of linoleum.

□ Make a hole for the jump rings in the center of each end of the rectangles about 5mm ($\frac{1}{4}''$) from the edge. Set aside 28 strips with only one hole for the last piece of each strip. If using vinyl flooring make small holes with punch. If using linoleum, support it on a piece of wood and pierce it with a bradawl or nail with a blow from the hammer.

□ To make the jump rings coil the wire around a tubular shape with a diameter of about 2.5cm (1")—a broom handle will do. (See Metal 1 p25).

□ Remove the coil of wire from the tube and, using the cutters, cut along the length of the coil to separate the rings. You will need 364 jump rings of 2.5cm (1") diameter and 28 of 4cm ($1\frac{1}{2}''$) diameter to thread onto the dowel rod.

□ To link the rectangles slip the jump rings through the holes and close them with the pliers. Each completed strip should start with a large jump ring and finish with a rectangle which has only one hole in it.

As the size of the curtain will vary according to the size of the door you want to cover, you can do the work in stages until you have enough strips to cover the required size.

□ Slip the dowel through the large jump rings and fix the curtain above the door in the same way as you would an ordinary curtain (fig. 1).

□ If using linoleum or vinyl flooring, you can either paint the rough side before cutting/or/glue aluminum foil to it. The curtain then looks attractive on both sides.

Other ways to use jump rings

You can link a series of jump rings or metal disks to form a chain-mail firescreen or a deep fringe around a big metal lampshade. If the jump rings are neat enough they can be joined to make a belt or even a change purse.

Victoria Drew

1. *Slip dowel through large jump rings.*

Left: assembling tools and equipment.
Right: the completed door curtain is light and airy.

Sand candles and garden flares

Wax 2

Make evening garden parties glow with flares, stabbed firmly into grass or earth. They are made by building up a candle on a wick by pouring molten wax down the wick—the same process used for making long church candles.

To make a flare

For one flare
You will need:
A 45cm (18″) length of 2.5cm (1″) wick
200 gm (½lb) powdered paraffin wax
25 gm (1oz) stearin
A piece of cotton cloth, 50cm x 12.5 cm (20″x5″)
A 45cm (18″) length of bamboo cane, 1.25cm (½″) in diameter
Scotch tape
Wax dye if required

☐ Melt stearin with dye (if you want a colored candle) and add paraffin wax. When it has melted, put the wick into the molten wax, then remove it, allowing the drips to fall back into the pan. When the wick has cooled a little, pull it taut, allowing it to stiffen.

☐ Heat the wax to 71°C (160°F) then, using a tablespoon and holding the wick over the pan, spoon the molten wax down the wick. Don't have the wax too hot as it will re-melt the wax already built up on the candle and so will take longer to make.

☐ Spoon the wax around the wick about once a minute, rotating the wick between forefinger and thumb so that you get an even coat all over the wick. You may have to reheat the wax about every 10 minutes — remember to keep it on a low flame.

☐ You can run the candle under the cold faucet to speed up the process but wipe the candle well with a tissue, as water trapped in the candle will make it splutter when burning.

☐ As the candle gets bigger it may require 3 or more spoonfuls at a time. Build it up to about 2cm (¾″) thick. If it is knobby, lightly roll it out on a clean, smooth, cool surface while it is still warm to get rid of unevenness. Leave it flat to cool and harden.

☐ Split the bamboo into 4 for about 12cm (5″) down from one end. Holding it open, push the candle base in, being careful not to cut your hands on the sharp edges of the bamboo; stick the candle to the bamboo with Scotch tape.

☐ Put the cotton cloth into the remainder of the wax in the pot and heat slowly. When the cloth has absorbed the wax, unfold it over the pan, allowing the drips to fall back into the pan. When it has stopped dripping, wrap the cloth tightly around the candle, and lay it on its side to dry.

Flare candles on bamboo stalks to light gardens or patios. Designed by David Constable.

Like dipped candles and rolled beeswax candles, sand candles do not require a mold. All that's necessary is an object that can make a clear-cut hole in sand. An ash-tray, ornament, jello mold, the bottom of a bottle, jar or bowl — any of these will do.

You will need:
Paraffin wax
Stearin
Dye (optional)
Thermometer
Sand
A bucket or box for the sand
An object to make the shape
Wick: choose one that leaves at least 2.5cm (1″) of wax unburned. For instance, if the candle is 7.5cm (3″) in diameter, put in a 5cm (2″) wick
A wicking needle: this is for making the hole for the wick through the partially set wax in the sand

☐ Fill a bucket or box with clean, damp sand and smooth off the surface to make it absolutely level without packing it down. Don't have a little bit of sand in the bottom of a deep box as you will not be able to impress the mold firmly enough.

☐ Dig a hole in the center of the sand, push your mold into it, then remove the mold. If the sand is too wet the hole will not keep its shape, nor will enough sand cling to the wax.

Pushing the mold into the sand.

☐ Add stearin and dye to the paraffin wax and heat it in a pan to 250°F (121°C).

☐ Cut a length of wick to the depth of the candle; prime it by dipping it into the wax and pulling it straight.

☐ Pour the wax carefully into the shape in the sand. You may find it easier at first to pour the wax into a pitcher and from there into the hole. But remember that the hotter the wax the more sand is picked up; at 250°F (121°C) between 1.5cm (½″) and 2.5cm (1″) is picked up. If a thicker sand wall is required, the wax should be even

Dick Miller

Melvin Grey

hotter. As the wax cools, the level in the sand will drop; refill the hole as necessary, keeping the temperature of the new wax high.

Remove the mold carefully.

☐ Allow the sand candle to harden in a cold place for one or two hours. After this time, push the wicking needle down the center and leave it standing upright.

Pouring the wax into the sand mold.

☐ Leave the candle overnight and dig it out the next day, loosening the sand around it carefully and brushing away any loose sand.
☐ Remove the needle and insert the already waxed wick into the hole.
☐ Top up around the wick hole with melted wax at 220°F (104°C) and allow it to set.
☐ Carve away areas of sand to make a design, being careful not to dig too deeply into the wax. If the right wick is chosen, the sand shell will remain intact after the candle has burned out and can be refilled with new wax.

Colorful sand candles have biscuit-like crusts. Designed by David Constable.

Dick Miller

Drawing a heart accurately

A heart is one of the most difficult shapes to draw freehand, since it must be symmetrical or it will look unbalanced. If you use the following methods, however, you will be able to draw the heart illustrated accurately in any size you want—and we have included hints on how, with a little practice, you can make other hearts with different proportions.

You will need:
A compass, or string and pencil
Ruler and pencil

☐ First you must decide what size you want the heart to be. The instructions refer to 'units', which are $\frac{1}{12}$ of the total height. Decide what size a unit should be and use the same proportions as given here. The heart will be fractionally taller than it is wide, but when deciding what size it should be, you can consider the height and width to be the same.

☐ Draw a vertical line (AB) 12 units long, which will run up the middle of the heart. Mark off a point C, 2 units from A, and a point D, 3 units from A. Make a right angle at D and extend this line so you now have a cross.

☐ Set the span of your compass to 3 units, put the pin at C and draw 2 small arcs to cut the cross-line at E and F. Now put the pin at E and F in turn and draw 2 arcs to connect C and the cross-line (fig.1).

☐ Set the span of your compass to 8 units, place the pin on the cross-line, 8 units in from where one of the first arcs cuts it, and draw an arc. Repeat on the other side (fig.2).

☐ Finally, draw 2 lines from B as tangents to the last 2 arcs, ie so that they will touch the arcs but will not cut them even if extended (fig.3). These lines complete the heart with a point at the bottom.

Other heart shapes

You can make lots of different hearts with the same basic method. For a thinner shape, you can make the radius of the top arcs smaller (fig.4). Or you could draw the cross-line farther down, so that AD becomes, say, 4 units instead of 3. Or make the radius of the top arcs bigger for a plumper heart.

If you want to avoid the straight lines, you should draw curves instead of the bottom tangents, using 2 more arcs with a radius of, say, 14 units (fig.5). If you decide to use another pair of arcs—or even more—be careful to align them to make a smooth join. You should be able to draw a straight line connecting the centers from which you drew each arc and the point where they meet (fig.6).

Trial and error is the best way of 'personalizing' your hearts—draw some hearts freehand to see what shape you prefer and then adjust the method accordingly.

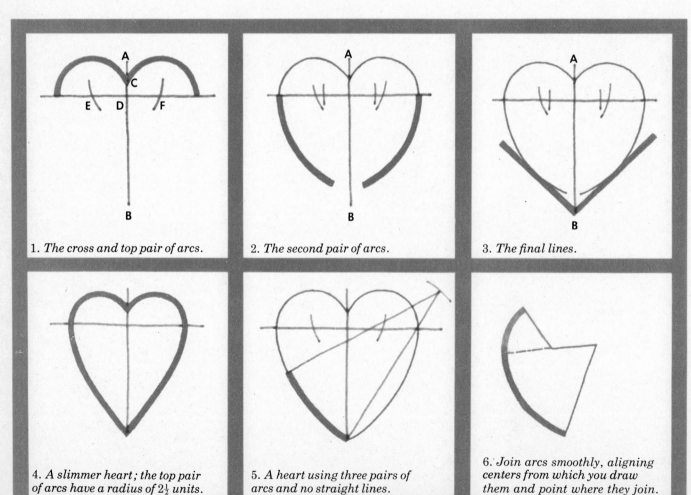

1. *The cross and top pair of arcs.*

2. *The second pair of arcs.*

3. *The final lines.*

4. *A slimmer heart; the top pair of arcs have a radius of $2\frac{1}{2}$ units.*

5. *A heart using three pairs of arcs and no straight lines.*

6. *Join arcs smoothly, aligning centers from which you draw them and point where they join.*

Victoria Drew

Creative ideas 3

Steve Bicknell

Take a lucky dip

Working with resin film is one of the simplest and most economical crafts; all you need is some copper or galvanized wire and a can of resin film. Optional extras: scraps of chenille-covered wire or colored pipe cleaners for stamens or insect bodies; green plastic or crepe paper for covering stems.

How it's done. Cut a length of wire and bend it into shape. A clematis petal, for example, will take about 25cm (10″) of wire but allow a little more than the finished circumference so that you have a stem to hold the flower by when dipping and then drying.

Twist the ends of the wire together or cross them to form a closed shape. Holding the shape by this stem, dip it quickly in and out of the resin (not too quickly or bubbles will appear on the surface of the film). Turn it up immediately so that the resin flows back toward the stem. This forms a barely visible vein down the center —just right for leaves or butterflies' wings.

Draw the edge of the shape across the can to wipe off the excess resin, then jab the stem into a potato or a piece of polystyrene to dry; this will take only a few minutes

For a flower, make a number of petals in the same way and twist their stems together at the back.

To form the crinkly edge of leaves or petals, curl the center of the piece of wire around and around a knitting or darning needle.

Mix colors to make different shades. For a lighter tone, add a little clear resin to the chosen color; for a darker shade, dip several times.

Variegated leaves and wings can be made by dripping a little of one color on top of another and then dipping through both layers.

To dip something that is taller than the depth of the tin, pour the resin into a tall vessel and tilt it. You can pour the excess resin back into the cans but it will thicken. Peel off any resin clinging to the vessel—or yourself—when it has dried. A can will last a long time if you remember to replace the lid tightly. If the resin hardens add a teaspoonful of thinner.

Finishing touches. For flower centers, cut a piece of yellow chenille wire and stick it with a dab of resin to the center of the made-up flower.

For standing flowers, twist a stem of thicker wire around the petal stems at the back and cover with green plastic or crepe paper. For the bee and dragonfly wind chenille wire around a finger to make the shape, then stick on wings.

Make the butterfly similarly but add wire antennae and spots to the wings.

Very important: resin is inflammable so don't smoke while you're working.

Butterflies, bees, flowers— just dip and leave to dry.

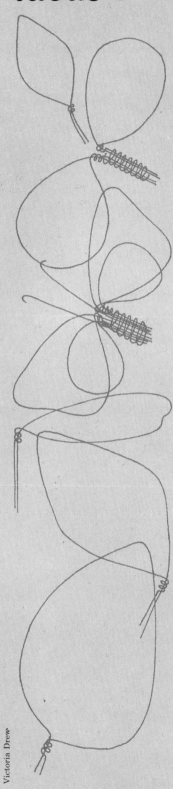

Victoria Drew

Cut lengths of wire and bend into a variety of shapes— petals, leaves and butter- flies are all simple to make. Add chenille-covered wire for bodies and flower centers.

Making tissue paper flowers

Artificial flowers are not new; the beauty of real flowers has always been a source of fascination and attempts to copy them over the years have been ingenious and varied. All sorts of different materials have been used, including wax, shells, glass, china, wood, felt, wool and many different kinds of fabric and paper.

Artificial flowers are now most commonly made in paper—they are easy to make and have great decorative appeal, and there is still scope for those with a serious interest in flowers to achieve accurate results.

Look at a real flower

Before beginning to make flowers, it is important to know how real ones are constructed. For a cross-section of the components of a flower, showing the main parts together with their proper names, see fig.1.

Although you can make satisfactory and decorative flowers by learning some useful papercraft techniques, you may want to go a stage further and make some that are closely copied from nature. It is then important to know exactly how a flower is formed by taking it apart and noting the exact number of petals and where they are

placed, the shape of the calyx and the distribution of the stamens. Whatever kind of flower you are making, it is a good idea to incorporate some accurate botanical details—they make the flower more interesting and subtle.

Tissue paper

Tissue is ideal for the beginner. It gives good results without requiring a great deal of expertise in handling, and the colors available are pretty enough to give the flowers the glow and fragility of real ones. A 'rainbow' variety is also available which gives an attractive effect to flower petals. The quality of tissue paper varies from flimsy to firm: it is worth buying the best available because it gives better, more long-lasting results. Tissue paper does have certain disadvantages, however, in comparison with the initially more difficult to handle crepe paper. It cannot be shaped in the same way, and if it becomes over-handled or crumpled it may lose its bright crispness. It also fades rather quickly when exposed to sunlight, so arrange the completed flowers in an attractive container placed well back from the window, and direct some lamplight through them in the evening. Be careful not to get tissue paper wet; even a few spots of water can cause the dye to run and spoil the paper.

Flower-making equipment

The only other materials required are wire and stem covering. Florists' wire is a very fine wire used for securing the flower to the stem, and galvanized wire in various thicknesses is used for stems. Wire stems can be covered with strips of green crepe paper, but rubber garden tape can also be used.

Only the most basic equipment is necessary—a pair of good quality sharp, pointed scissors with a blade

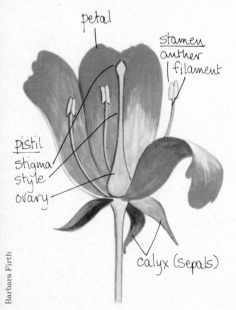

1. Cross section through a composite flower, showing the main parts.

Add a splash of color to dark walls with pompom paper flowers. Fill a pitcher with flowers on covered stems and place against a contrasting background. While making the flowers, pin individual blooms directly to a wall to prevent them getting crumpled. From a kit designed by Priscilla Lobley.

Barbara Firth

Melvin Grey

about 6cm (2½″) long, a pair of wire cutters (the sort used for electrical repairs) and a general purpose glue.

To make tissue peonies

Peonies are large, striking flowers that vary in color from yellow, white and magenta to all shades of pink and red. The dark red varieties are the most familiar, but there are delicate two-shaded flowers in tones of white and gold, pink and cream and pale and deep pink that look particularly subtle made up in tissue paper.

You will need:

For 2 flowers you will need 2 sheets of tissue paper, each in a different shade, such as magenta and lemon or pink and cream.

25cm-35cm (10″-15″) of 1.25mm (18 Gauge) galvanized wire.

Florists' wire or green plastic-covered wire. Green crepe paper.

General purpose glue or paste

☐ Cut off the required number of galvanized wire lengths for stems and straighten them out.

☐ Each sheet of tissue paper measures about 50cm x 74cm (20″x30″). Divide each sheet into 6 equal squares by folding the paper in half and then into 3 (fig.1a). For each flower you will need 3 squares of one shade for the center petals and 3 squares of the other color for the outer petals.

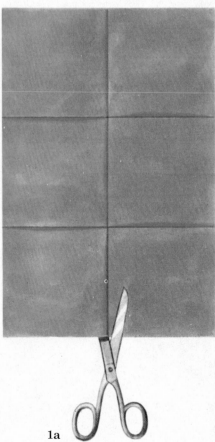

1a. *Dividing a whole sheet of tissue paper into six equal squares.*

87

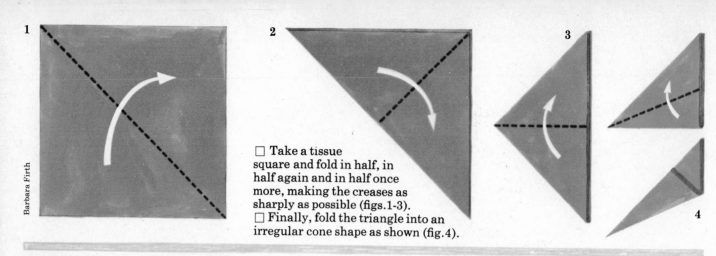

1

2

☐ Take a tissue square and fold in half, in half again and in half once more, making the creases as sharply as possible (figs.1-3).
☐ Finally, fold the triangle into an irregular cone shape as shown (fig.4).

3

4

Barbara Firth

Final flower head in subtle shades.

☐ The next step makes the shape of the petals, so be careful to make the cut exactly as shown (fig.5). Cutting line A indicates the shape of the inside petals, cutting line B the outside petals. Cut 3 of each.

A   **B**

5

☐ Spread out the petals but do not flatten them (fig.6). Dab a spot of glue on to the center of each of the petals (fig.7) and place them one on top of each other (fig.8), being careful to keep the creases in.

6   **7**   **8**

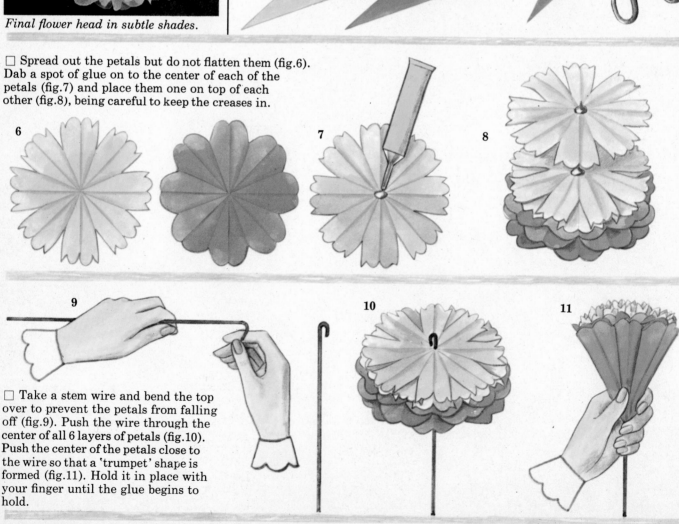

9

☐ Take a stem wire and bend the top over to prevent the petals from falling off (fig.9). Push the wire through the center of all 6 layers of petals (fig.10). Push the center of the petals close to the wire so that a 'trumpet' shape is formed (fig.11). Hold it in place with your finger until the glue begins to hold.

10   **11**

□ Secure base of flower by binding tightly with Florists' or green plastic-covered wire (fig.12). Shape the flower by gently separating each of the layers of outer petals and turning them downward, and by separating the inner petals and leaving them standing vertically (fig.13).

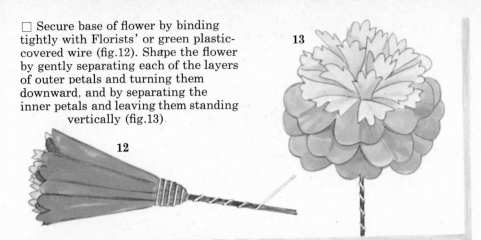

□ Cover the stem wire by cutting a strip of green crepe paper about 2.5cm (1") wide and wrapping it very tightly around the base of the flower. A dab of glue on the end of the paper may help to hold it in position (fig.14).

□ Rotate the wire, and wrap paper strip in a bandaging movement down to the bottom of the wire (fig.15). Break off the paper and secure the end with a dab of glue (fig.16).

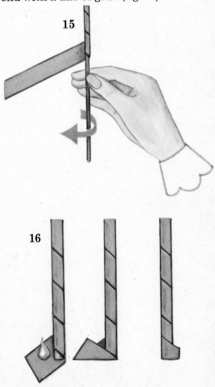

Delicate tissue paper peonies designed by Priscilla Lobley.

Slab pottery picture tiles

As well as being patted or sliced into a square block, clay can also be rolled out flat, rather like pastry. Clay sheets rolled out in this way are called slabs, and potters use them to build slab pots and dishes, to make sculptures and geometrical constructions.

The slab, because it is so easy to make, is an excellent form for the beginner to work with. Once rolled out to an even thickness, the clay can be cut into several tiles with a sharp knife, and other slabs of varying thickness can be trimmed and pressed on to the clay surface to give a relief effect. Like the block, the slab can be painted, impressed with objects or modeled upon.

Making a clay slab

Using an ordinary wooden rolling pin and a flat surface such as a wooden table top, covered with burlap or canvas, begin by flattening a ball of clay (fig.1) and rolling out so that it makes a rough oval (fig.2).

The clay can finally be rolled so that it is an even thickness all over by placing it between two flat strips of wood, each as thick as the required depth of the slab, and then rolling it with the ends of the rolling pin resting on the wooden strips (fig.3).

Two cheap wooden rulers glued together, for example, give a 6mm ($\frac{1}{4}''$) strip which is a useful thickness for tiles and similar shapes.

The resulting slab is now completely even, and the same thickness as the strips. Ease away the burlap (fig.4) as shown.

Relief modeling on a tile

The landscape tile shown here is a simple relief project that can be made in either natural or self-hardening clay. Follow these techniques to build up your own landscape, whether it is real or imagined.

To make a relief tile

You will need:
$\frac{3}{8}$kg ($\frac{3}{4}$lb) clay
Poster paints for decorating
Clear varnish, if required
Sharp knife; wooden ruler; rolling pin; 2 sticks about 6mm ($\frac{1}{4}''$) thick for rolling out clay; plastic sheeting.

□ Roll out the clay evenly to a thickness of 6mm ($\frac{1}{4}''$) to accommodate your tile shape. Measure and mark out the tile on the rolled-out clay, using a torn-off corner of newspaper to give the right angles.

□ To cut the tile lay the ruler along the edges of the tile and, using this and the newspaper as a guide, trim away the sides of the tile with the sharp knife (fig.5). To do this, slide the knife through the clay from one corner to half way along one edge of the clay then remove it. Then slide it again from the opposite corner. If you slice straight along the edge you will stretch the clay out of shape. Keep the trimmed off pieces to build up the picture.

□ Cut out a series of curving shapes to represent mountain and valley formations.

□ Build up the scene gradually, starting with the background masses and positioning more shapes on top of them so that the foreground is in the highest relief. Stick each land mass into place by teasing the back of it with an old toothbrush dipped in water. Tease the clay area on to which it is to be fixed in the same way and press the relief slab firmly into position with the fingertips.

□ When the landscape is complete, place it on a sheet of newspaper, cover with a sheet of plastic, and leave it to dry out slowly and thoroughly.

□ When the tile is quite dry, paint it with poster colors. It is worth remembering that, unless you are a proficient painter, more striking effects are achieved with a few simple colors. As a general rule, paint the foreground high-reliefs in paler shades, toning down to dark colors in the distance. If desired, the completed tile can finally be painted with clear varnish or polyurethane lacquer to give it a glossy finish.

Right: landscape tile that makes an ideal first modeling project. Designed by Val Barry.

1. *Begin by flattening a square block of clay, using a wooden rolling pin.*

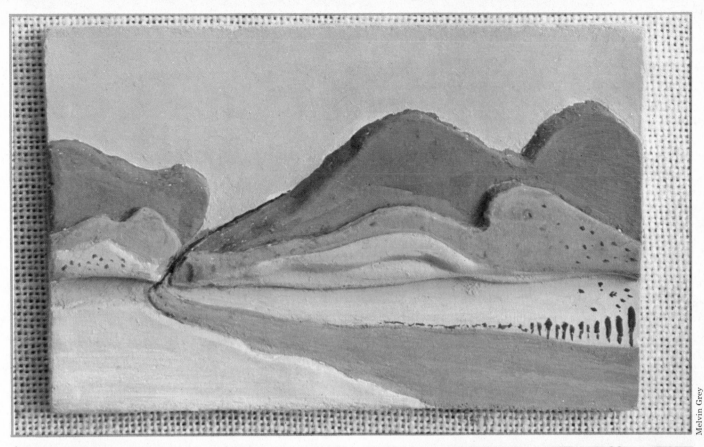

Melvin Grey

2. *First rolling—to flatten the clay into a rough oval.*

4. *Easing the burlap away from the clay for next stage.*

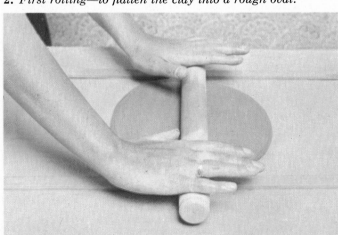

3. *Rolling in second direction to an even thickness, using two flat sticks as a guide.*

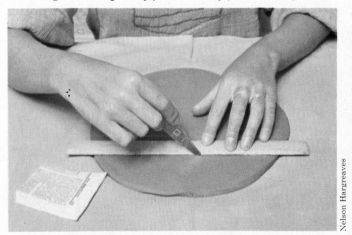

Nelson Hargreaves

5. *Measuring and cutting clay tile, using ruler as guide and a scrap of newspaper to give accurate right angles.*

To make the face tile

The relief modeled picture is one way in which the basic tile can be decorated. As another idea, try your own version of the stylized face picture shown here, or try making an abstract panel.

Colored stains in the form of special colored powders for staining clay or coloring glazes have been used. As the pigment is expensive, it is best to keep initial projects small—about 20cm x 30cm (8"x12")—as in the picture here. Choose 3 or 4 clay stains, remembering that fewer colors look more effective than a confusing variety, when combined with the texture of the clay.

Clay stained with colored powders.

You will need:

1kg (2lb) clay

Colored stains (colored powders for staining clay or coloring glazes). Flat wooden board or table; wooden rolling pin; 2 sticks about 6mm ($\frac{1}{4}$") thick for rolling out clay; steel ruler; sharp knife; tracing paper; plastic sheeting; clear varnish, if required

Nails, screws and hairpins, or other small objects for texturing clay

Thin layer of sponge or foam, large enough to cover the picture

Heavy book, large enough to cover the picture

☐ Select one pale shade for the tile base, and mix about 4 teaspoons of powder with enough water to dissolve it completely. Work this mixture into a 700gm (1½lb) ball of clay until the color is evenly spread.

☐ For the applied decorations prepare small quantities of clay, about the same size as a pingpong ball, in the same way. Keep the different colored balls of clay separate, and make sure that the clay stays moist by covering it with sheets of plastic.

The face picture is built up from tiny balls of different colored clays pressed onto the surface of the tile. The resulting technique is intricate and delicate. Designed by Zuzanna Kleczkowski.

Two mirrors in soft, terracotta colored clay are another example of decorative slab work. The clay is sliced into attractive shapes, and a central portion is cut out so that the slab can be backed with mirror. Impressed and incised patterns complete the effect. Designed by The Birchwood Pottery.

☐ Trace face shape given here and draw to scale (Design Know-how 4, page 112), keeping a margin of at least 5cm (2") all around the picture.

☐ Roll the base clay out to an even 6mm ($\frac{1}{4}$") thickness. Patches of contrasting color in the base clay are obtained by placing blobs of different color on the tile, and rolling them in at the same time. It is best not to try to control where these areas merge but to let them find their own shape and position.

☐ Place the traced picture on the tile, and hold the corners in place with four small lumps of clay. Using a pencil, trace the design quickly onto the tile.

☐ Discard the paper and use a steel ruler and sharp knife to trim waste clay away from the picture.

☐ To apply the color make clay beads by pinching off tiny pieces of clay in the different colors, and rolling them with the fingertips in the palm of your hand. It is easiest to build up the lines that form the picture first and then to fill in the areas of color, so begin by pressing the beads in along the lines, and build up the solid areas gradually.

☐ Texture can be introduced after the beads have been applied with a pencil end, a matchstick, nail head or any other suitable shape.

☐ When the picture is finished, cover it with the foam and a heavy book, which will stop the clay warping as it dries out. When the picture is completely dry, finish it off with a coat of varnish.

☐ To hang the picture tile, screw a hook to a small square of wood and glue the wood to the tile with tile cement glue (fig.6).

6. Attach the hook with a screw to a piece of wood about 2.5cm (1") square, 6mm ($\frac{1}{4}$") thick.

Starting with simple stitches

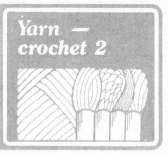
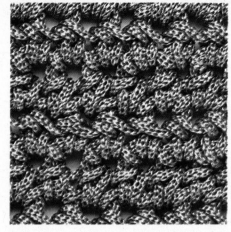

This chapter introduces two simple stitches—single crochet and half double crochet—which you can use to make up these pretty pillows and rag rug. Use heavy rayon, raffia or ribbon for effective pillows and odd pieces of cotton fabric for the rug.

Abbreviations
(for other abbreviations, see Crochet 1, page 38)
sc single crochet
hdc half double crochet

This close-up of a fabric made in half double crochet shows the texture of the stitch. Yarn used: Atlas Novacord.

Steve Bicknell

To work a single crochet

Start by making the number of chain stitches you need, adding one extra chain stitch—this acts as a turning chain, which is needed at the beginning of every row of single crochet to bring the hook up to the right height for working the first stitch.

1st row. Insert the hook from front to back into the third chain stitch from the hook (fig.1).

*Wind the yarn around the hook (fig.2) . . .

. . . and draw the loop through the chain stitch (fig.3).

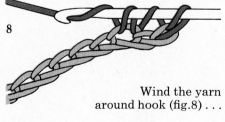

Wind the yarn around the hook and draw through both loops on the hook* (fig.4).

One single crochet has been made, plus first skipped 2 chain stitches which count as first single crochet, leaving one loop on hook. Insert hook into next chain stitch and repeat from * to * into each chain stitch to end.

On next and every following row, turn the work so that the yarn is again in position at the beginning of the row, make one chain stitch to count as first single crochet, skip first single crochet of previous row, work one single crochet into next single crochet.

When working into a previous row, unless otherwise stated, insert hook under top 2 loops of single crochet (fig.5).

Continue working single crochet into each single crochet to end, working the last single crochet under the turning chain of the previous row.

Half double crochet

Make the number of chain stitches you need, then add one extra chain stitch to count as a turning chain.

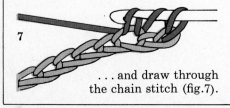

1st row. Wind the yarn around hook, insert hook from front to back into third chain stitch from hook, *wind the yarn around hook (fig.6).

. . . and draw through the chain stitch (fig.7).

Wind the yarn around hook (fig.8) . . .

. . . and draw through all 3 loops on hook* (fig.9).

One half double crochet has been made plus first skipped 2 chain stitches which count as first half double crochet, leaving one loop on hook. Wind the yarn around the hook, insert the hook into next chain stitch and repeat from * to * into each chain stitch to end.

On next and every following row, turn the work so that the yarn is again in position at the beginning of the row, make 2 chain stitches to count as first half double crochet skip first half double crochet of previous row, work one half double crochet into each half double crochet to end, inserting hook under top 2 loops (fig.5) and working the last half double crochet under the turning chain in the previous row.

Barbara Firth

Mini pillows

For pillow about 23cm (9″) square worked in half double crochet (or double crochet and single crochet).

You will need:

100gm (4oz) of tubular rayon macramé cord, raffia, or very narrow ribbon.

One No.7.00 ISR (US size K) crochet hook

23cm (9″) square pillow form made from muslin and stuffed

Using No.7.00 ISR (US size K) hook make enough ch to make 23cm (9″), about 22ch, which includes one extra ch to count as turning ch.

1st row. Into third ch from hook work 1hdc, then 1hdc into each ch to end. Turn. If you had 22ch to start with you should now have 21hdc.

2nd row. 2ch to count as first hdc, skip first hdc, 1hdc into each hdc to end, working the last hdc under the turning ch of the previous row. Rep second row until work measures 46cm (18″) from beg. Fasten off.

Finishing

Fold work in half WS tog and join 2 side edges with a sl/st (see Crochet chapter 1, page 37). Insert pillow form. Join rem edge.

Rag rug

This rug, measuring 2.6m x 1.3m (8′8″x 4′4″) is another example of using materials other than crochet yarns. If you have a lot of scrap cotton fabric in a ragbag you can tear it up into strips about 2cm (¾″) wide. Wind up the strips into balls, separating the colors. Work two or three rows with one color then change to another to build up a pleasing pattern.

Because the rug is worked in strips it is easy to handle while working.

If you don't feel like attempting a rug, use slightly thinner strips of fabric— say 1.5cm (½″)—to make country-style table mats.

You will need:

For rug 1.3m (4′4″) wide, lengths of cotton fabric in 4 colors. The total

This practical rag rug uses strips of colorful cotton material.

amount of material will depend on the length of rug required and the way which stripes of colors are arranged, 5.5m (6yd) of 90cm (36″) wide fabric will work out at about 76cm (30″) in length. One No.7.00 ISR (US size K) crochet hook

Button twist

1st strip. Using No.7.00 ISR (US size K) hook and any color, make enough ch to make 33cm (13″) width, about 27ch should be right, which includes one ch for turning.

1st row. Into third ch from hook work 1sc, then 1sc into each ch to end. Turn.

If you had 27ch to start with you should now have 26sc.

2nd row. 1ch to count as first sc, skip first sc, 1sc into each sc to end,

Lots of mini pillows make any chair comfortable. They are made in several yarns of subtle fall colors.

working the last sc under the turning ch of the previous row. Turn.

Rep second row for required length, changing colors as required and working over the ends each time a new strip is joined in, to secure them.

2nd strip. Make enough ch (about 19 should be right including 1ch for turning) to make 23cm (9″) width.

3rd strip. Make enough ch (about 35 should be right including 1ch for turning) to make 43cm (17″) width.

4th strip. Work as given for first strip to make 33cm (13″) width.

Finishing

Sew strips together with button twist.

Shirred top and skirt

Shirring

Shirring is both decorative and practical. Based on an elasticated yarn, it holds in fullness and is self adjusting to many sizes—very useful for clothes for growing children. Shirring yarn, which is widely available, is sold in spools and has a fine elastic core around which a cotton or rayon thread is wound.

The yarn is wound on the bobbin of a machine and lies on the underside of the work while stitching is worked from the right side (fig.1).

Modern sewing machines will have instructions for using shirring yarns

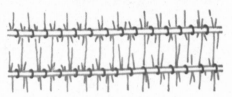

1. *Back view of shirring.*

which you should follow. If yours is an old machine you will have to experiment to find the best way of using it. You may find it best to wind the shirring yarn tightly on to the bobbin by hand. Loosen the bobbin tension slightly. The upper tension should be sufficiently slack to allow the elastic

yarn to go through the stitch loop without being drawn up into the fabric. Stitch, with right side of garment uppermost, using a slightly longer stitch length than for straight sewing. Work rows about 12mm to 24mm ($\frac{1}{2}''$ to $1''$) apart. At the end of a row, pull the threads through to the wrong side and knot each thread securely to avoid the threads slipping back.

If the garment is too large after shirring, draw up the elastic thread to take away more fullness.

Preparing a hem

Here are some basic rules which should be followed whenever you make a hem. Mark the hem line, then trim the hem allowance to an even width all around. Pin up the hem (fig.2). Always pin at

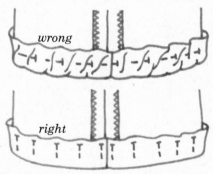

2. *Pinning up a hem.*

right angles to the hem. Never slant the pins or place them parallel to the hem as this can result in a shift in the layers of fabric, giving an unattractive twist in the finished hem.

Baste the hem about 12mm ($\frac{1}{2}''$) from the lower edge, using long basting stitches. Give the hem a light press, easing in any fullness around the raw edge.

Always press with the hem lying flat on the ironing board and the garment supported over the back of a chair.

Do not press too hard over the basting stitches as they might leave impressions in the cloth and always press the hem from the wrong side.

Be careful not to press right over the hem edge as this will leave an impression in the fabric.

Slip stitch

Slip stitch gives an invisible finish. Here a fold edge is being sewn to a flat

3
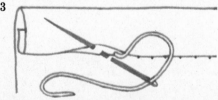

piece (fig.3). Take only one or two threads through the flat surface and a good deep stitch through the fold. Don't pull the stitches tight as this will show through to the right side.

The shirred top and skirt are ideal for informal evening wear.

Camera Press

Making the top and skirt

Back view of shirred top.

This shirred outfit is an ideal project for the beginner as shirring will accommodate any small discrepancies in the making up and virtually no fitting is required. The shirred top and skirt can be worn together or as separates—the simple top goes equally well with jeans or shorts and the skirt looks great with a T-shirt.

Use fine fabrics such as fine cottons, tricel, lurex or soft jersey to avoid a bulky garment.

Making the top

You will need:

115cm (45″) wide or 90cm (36″) wide fine fabric, 105cm (1yd)

Shirring yarn, matching thread

☐ Following figs. 4 and 5, cut out the fabric. For the bodice cut two rectangles of fabric 40.8cm (16″) deep and each to the width of your bust measurement, so that the total width of fabric is twice your size.

For straps cut two strips of fabric each 45cm x 9cm (18″x3½″).

☐ On each rectangle turn under 6mm (¼″) all around and stitch close to fold.

☐ With right sides together, taking 12mm (½″) seams, join the rectangles together down both 40.8cm (16″) sides. Press seams open.

☐ Turn under top edge 30mm (1¼″), baste and press. Repeat on lower edge.

☐ Starting at one side seam, work a row of shirring around bodice 24mm (1″) from top edge. Then work your shirring around bodice at 12mm (½″) intervals to 24mm (1″) from lower

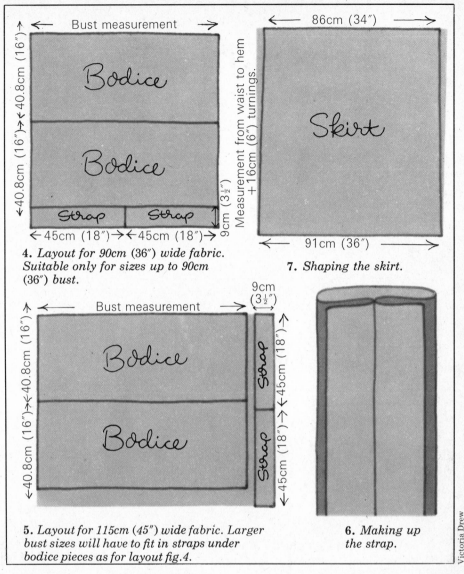

4. Layout for 90cm (36″) wide fabric. Suitable only for sizes up to 90cm (36″) bust.

7. Shaping the skirt.

5. Layout for 115cm (45″) wide fabric. Larger bust sizes will have to fit in straps under bodice pieces as for layout fig.4.

6. Making up the strap.

Victoria Drew

edge. The top and bottom rows of shirring will secure the hems.

☐ Pull thread ends to inside and knot. Try on garment. If too loose pull up shirring elastic to fit and tie again.

☐ Fold one strap in half along the length, with right sides together. Taking a 12mm (½″) seam, stitch long edges. Press seam open with the seam positioned at center of strap (fig.6). Turn to right side and press again. Make up other strap in the same way.

☐ Try on top and position straps in most comfortable position. Trim straps to correct length and even ends. Stitch firmly to the top along the first line of shirring.

Making the skirt

You will need:

90cm (36″) wide fine fabric, twice your length from waist to hem plus 16cm (6″) for turnings

Shirring yarn, matching thread

☐ Cut two pieces of fabric to your length from waist to hem plus 8cm (3″). Taper each piece to 86cm (34″) at waist edge (fig.7).

☐ Taking 24mm (1″) seams, stitch side seams and even seam allowances.

☐ Turn in waist edge 6mm (¼″) and machine stitch close to fold. Turn in again 18mm (¾″), baste and press.

☐ Starting at one side seam, work a row of shirring around skirt 12mm (½″) down from waist edge. This will secure the top hem.

☐ Continue working rows of shirring 12mm (½″) apart for 12cm (5″). Knot the ends then try on skirt. Some figures may find 18cm (7″) more flattering or, for a very thin figure, 20cm (8″) may be more suitable. So work the required number of rows, pull threads through to wrong side and knot. Tighten shirring yarn if necessary.

☐ Pin up hem to correct length. For a machine stitched hem, trim hem allowance to 12mm (½″). Turn in raw edge for 6mm (¼″). Baste hem and machine stitch close to fold.

For a hand-sewn hem, trim seam allowance to 36mm (1½″). Turn in raw edge 12mm (½″), baste and press, then slip stitch hem in place.

Improvised printing blocks

There are many different ways of printing and perhaps one of the simplest and most effective is printing from found objects—things that give a ready-made design that can be found around the house or in the garden.

There are many things which will print just as they are, needing no preparation. If the object, such as a leaf, is intricate and beautiful in itself, one single print may be best. If it is less interesting on its own then an endless variety of patterns can be made by repeating the printed impression. The arrangement of these impressions may be random or ordered into lines, crossing lines or checks.

The examples shown here have been printed with poster paint, printing water colors, and oil-bound printing ink.

Water solvent paints

Poster paint has the disadvantage of drying up while you are printing and also tends to go into blobs, but this can add its own effective character to the print. It is best to use poster paint (or powder paint) diluted with very little water and applied with a stiff hog-hair brush.

Printing water colors do not dry so quickly and give a more faithful impression of the printing object. They may also be applied with a stiff brush, having first been diluted with a little water.

Applying the color. To a certain extent the thing with which you are printing will dictate the way in which the color is applied. When printing with a hard, rigid object it is often best to spread the printing water color on a flat sponge with a knife. This then acts as a stamping pad. Poster paints should not be used in this way as they dry up too quickly.

Oil-bound printing inks

To record the greatest amount of detail use oil-bound printing ink which is best applied with a linoleum roller, available from most art shops. You will need a shiny, flat surface on which to roll out the ink, such as a piece of glass, a sheet of mirror or formica board.

Applying the color. Squeeze some ink on the glass in a line as long as the width of your roller. Roll this out in different directions until you have it evenly distributed. Don't spread it further than the area which the roller covers in a single revolution. It is wasteful to cover a larger area.

If you want to mix up a color for printing, blend the inks together with a palette knife at the side of the glass and roll out the new color. It is unsatisfactory to try to mix the colors by simply rolling them together.

If you buy fabric printing oil-bound inks you can use them on both paper and cloth. Printing water colors may also be used on both materials.

Preparing to print

Before you start printing have ready some newsprint for test prints, the paper or cloth you plan to print on (which has been cut to the size required) and rags for cleaning up and wiping your hands. If you are using oil-bound inks you will need some turpentine for cleaning up afterward. Be sure you have ample space in which to put the wet prints. You could erect a temporary line with large clips or clothes pins from which to hang the prints.

It is a good idea to experiment with the amount of ink deposited on the paper. Fig.1 shows a repeat pattern using printing water color on the end of a cotton spool. Color was applied to the printing surface at every third print

The shapes of familiar objects can be seen in amazingly new and original ways when they are used as objects for printing. Try and guess the items used to print the patterns opposite:

cotton reel.
broom closet clip, heads of screws,
off-cut of wooden molding, paper doily,

1. *A cotton spool stamped repeatedly on paper makes a fascinating all-over pattern.*

Janet Allen

2

3

4

5. Leaf prints are very easy to do.

thus producing the variations in tone and texture. Don't feel you must strive for a perfect impression every time; with this method of printing this is not possible and the mottled, irregular textures that result generate their own interest.

Effects with different paints

Figs.2,3,4 show the different qualities of each type of paint or ink.

Fig.2 is a leaf printed with poster paint. Brush paint on to the back or more prominently veined side of the leaf. Lay the paper to be printed on a table with the painted leaf on top of it, paint side down, and place a piece of newspaper over the top (fig.5). Press down carefully on the newspaper, making sure

2, 3, 4. These images of oak leaves look more like an artist's interpretation than prints of the real thing. Different types of color give each print a special character. All designs by Janet Allen.

you cover all of the leaf. Pressure can also be applied with a clean roller.

Gently peel off the newspaper and the leaf from your print and hang it up to dry.

In fig.3 the leaf is printed in the same way as fig.2 but with printing watercolor, therefore there is more definition than with the poster paint.

Fig.4 shows a leaf printed with oil-bound printing ink, applied to the leaf with a roller. Detail is even clearer than with printing watercolor.

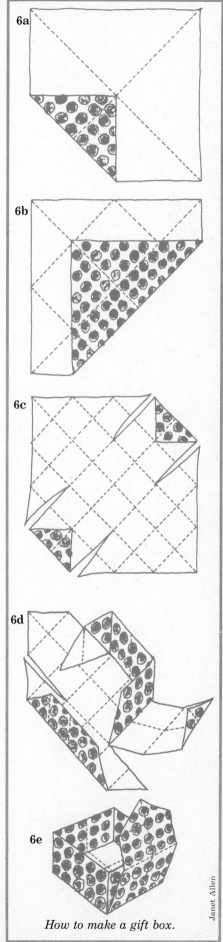

By printing and folding paper a pretty box can be produced to make gifts even more appealing.

To make the box

Decorated paper, besides making distinctive gift wrappings, can be used for shelf paper or to line the walls and back of the inside of a cupboard or bookshelf.

If you like to make gifts of home-made chocolate, candy, or fruit or vegetables from your garden, present them in a gift box also of your own making, printed with your own design.

The box shown here was made from paper printed with a cotton spool.

☐ To make the box cut a 36cm (14″) square of paper. Fold the diagonals, open out and then fold the corners into the center (fig.6a). Open out. You now have a square folded diagonally within the paper square.

☐ Now fold each corner to the far side of the inner square (fig.6b). Finally, fold each corner to the near side of the inner square (fig.6c).

☐ On one corner, make cuts two squares deep on either side of the center fold (fig.6c). Do the same on the corner opposite to this.

☐ Fold the two sides without cuts inwards along existing creases (fig.6d). Fold over the ends of these sides again. Fold the remaining two corners along existing creases and slot the ends under the ends of the previous two sides (fig.6e). This completes the box.

How to make a gift box.

Versatile shelf units

Perhaps the most enjoyable aspect of 'do-it-yourself' carpentry is the sheer satisfaction you get from creating something. So don't worry about the cracks and gaps and the slips of the saw—they form part of the interest and attraction of handmade articles and can usually be dealt with effectively.

Even after years of practice and using accurate machinery there will still be imperfections. Covering up the mistakes is as important to carpentry as sawing along a straight line. That is why there are base boards to cover up the untidy joins between the floor boards and the walls, and wood filler to patch up the bumps and bruises where the hammer missed its target.

In other words, don't worry about minor mistakes. There is usually some ingenious way you can cover them up. Anyway, it would be difficult to imagine a beginner sawing perfectly straight or hammering a nail without missing. A little practice will tell you which mistakes can be salvaged and also how to deal with them.

This project is almost as easy to make as the trivet in Carpentry chapter 1. The same basic principle of joining the pieces is used, but in this case the 'grid' is completed with a surrounding border which is nailed to the other pieces.

This storage unit can, of course, be made smaller or larger than the one described in the directions. And it can be used equally well as a bathroom cabinet, a desk tidy or as a kitchen spice rack.

If you are going to change the dimensions, it is advisable to plan it carefully by making full scale drawings be-

The storage unit as a purpose-built spice rack, designed by Alf Martensson.

fore starting to saw. Always work from the drawings.

Whereas the trivet called for enthusiasm and perhaps a little curiosity in beginning, this time perserverance and, as always, a little patience are useful. There are really only one or two steps, which must be repeated over and over again. But it will offer plenty of sawing practice. It is reassuring to remember that should some saw cuts be a little off and the holes a little too large, a small cover strip nailed to the face side will hide the gaps. Unfortunately it's more difficult to correct errors on the surrounding pieces. The corner joints, which in this case are the simplest possible, may be difficult to get just right. But this is a learning process and the important thing is that, after a few hours work, you have a useful and attractive spice rack and the satisfaction of knowing that you made it yourself.

Using a hammer

Hammer sizes are determined by the weight of the head. Try to use whichever hammer is available. But if buying one get one that is fairly light and comfortable. Most of the projects involve light nailing—i.e. using finishing nails with small heads that can be 'set' into the wood so that they don't show. To hammer a nail use two or three light taps with the hammer while holding the nail. Then use more force, with the fingers out of the way. If the wood surface will be exposed the nail should be driven almost flush with the surface. Don't make dents in the surface by continuing with the hammer if you want to 'hide the nails' below the surface. For this use a nail punch, or cheat a little and use a larger nail to sink the smaller one.

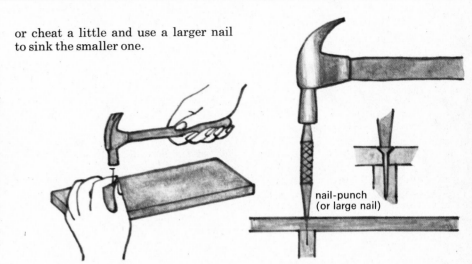

nail-punch
(or large nail)

To make the spice rack
You will need:

A piece of softwood 12mm x 75mm ($\frac{1}{2}$"x 3"), 3m (10') long, for grid interior

A piece of softwood 12mm x 100mm ($\frac{1}{2}$"x4"), 2m (6'6") long, for surrounding border

Finishing nails 19mm ($\frac{3}{4}$"), 3 dozen

12mm x 19mm ($\frac{1}{2}$"x$\frac{3}{4}$") beading or softwood strips, 2m (6'6") long (optional)

Fine sandpaper

When buying wood insist on selecting pieces which are straight and free from knots and splits. Very often, if wood is not adequately dried or if it hasn't been stored in the correct upright position, it will tend to warp, so sight down the piece of wood to check that it's fairly straight.

Remember the 12mm x 75mm ($\frac{1}{2}$"x3") or x 100mm (4") dimension is for wood as it is sawn from a large log. The planed size is slightly smaller since a few millimeters are taken off in the planing process. So when planning the sawing remember to measure the actual thickness carefully.

Tools:

Saw
Carpenter's square
Chisel 10mm ($\frac{3}{8}$")
Pencil
Hammer
Steel rule

These tools, with the exception of the hammer, were introduced in Carpentry chapter 1. They are all basic tools and should form part of any tool kit. But it should be emphasized that if one of these is not available it is not absolutely necessary to buy it. Try to improvise. For example, instead of a steel rule an ordinary ruler could be used; and it is possible to substitute a square-cornered piece of cardboard or even a book for a carpenter's square. All that is needed is an accurate 90° angle. Besides, there will be many times when you have misplaced or forgotten a tool. There is, however, no substitute for the saw.

☐ Cut the lengths required. First mark a line about 25mm (1") from the end with a carpenters' square and cut off to start with a 'square' end.

Measure the lengths, mark with carpenters' square, and saw along side of line.

☐ Sand all the pieces using a sanding block. Sandpaper comes in various grades from very coarse for rough work to very fine for finishing touches. Sand along the grain, otherwise scratches will show when the piece is finished.

☐ Mark the two 12mm x 75mm ($\frac{1}{2}$"x 3"), 48cm (19") long pieces as shown.

☐ Mark the six 12mm x 75mm ($\frac{1}{2}$"x3"), 30cm (12") long pieces as shown.

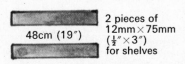

48cm (19")

2 pieces of
12mm × 75mm
($\frac{1}{2}$"×3")
for shelves

6 pieces of
12mm × 75mm
($\frac{1}{2}$"×3") for
vertical dividers

30cm
(12")

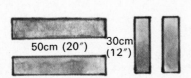

50cm (20")   30cm
(12")

4 pieces of 12mm×100mm ($\frac{1}{2}$"×4")
for border 2 pieces 50cm(20") long :
2 pieces 30cm(12") long

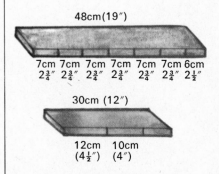

48cm(19")

7cm 7cm 7cm 7cm 7cm 7cm 6cm
2$\frac{3}{4}$" 2$\frac{3}{4}$" 2$\frac{3}{4}$" 2$\frac{3}{4}$" 2$\frac{3}{4}$" 2$\frac{3}{4}$" 2$\frac{1}{2}$"

30cm (12")

12cm   10cm
(4$\frac{1}{2}$")   (4")

Ken Wheatley

☐ When cutting out notches, instead of going through the tedious process of drawing all the lines halfway across each piece (see Carpentry chapter 1), make a cardboard template as shown.

☐ Place template along marks and mark the notches using a sharp pencil. Mark as shown.

☐ Check that the lines stop at exactly half the width and that the thickness is exactly that of the pieces of wood. Repeat for all six 30cm (12″) pieces and the two 48cm (19″) pieces.

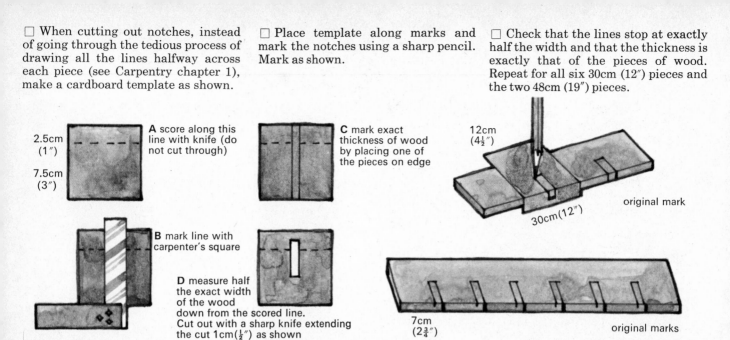

2.5cm (1″)
7.5cm (3″)

A score along this line with knife (do not cut through)

B mark line with carpenter's square

C mark exact thickness of wood by placing one of the pieces on edge

D measure half the exact width of the wood down from the scored line. Cut out with a sharp knife extending the cut 1cm(½″) as shown

12cm (4½″)

30cm(12″)

original mark

7cm (2¾″)

original marks

☐ Sawing on the inside of the line, cut all the pieces as shown.

☐ Using a chisel remove the wood pieces. Place chisel along line and, by pushing gently down, the pieces should come out easily. Square off the cut with the chisel.

☐ After having smoothed all the sawn edges with sandpaper, assemble the pieces.

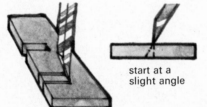

start at a slight angle

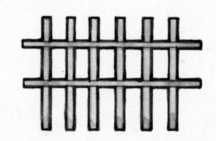

☐ Place the 12mm x 100mm (½″x4″), 30cm (12″) long pieces on the sides, with one edge flush with the back of the interlocking pieces. Sighting from the front, start nailing by tapping lightly with the hammer. The nails must be positioned so that when driven all the way in they will not stick out on the sides. Use two nails for each shelf.

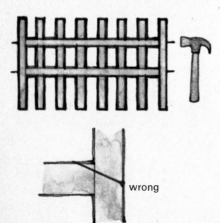

wrong

☐ Now place one of the last two pieces of 12mm x 100mm (½″x4″), 50cm (20″) long, on top and nail along each vertical section.

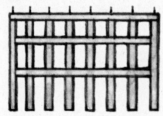

Do the same with bottom piece.
This is a good time to take a little survey and check whether there are any gaps or marks which can be fixed or covered over. You may find that the four corners do not fit perfectly. Unless this is particularly bothersome it is best to leave them and to make sure that you measure more carefully next time. If it's very bad, you can remove the larger piece and cut a bit off if it's too long. If it's too short the only remedy is to make a new piece.

Another possible place where errors can show noticeably is at the junctions of the grid pieces. If the sawcuts were not perfect (which they aren't usually) the only remedy is to cover them up. Strips of wood 12mm x 19mm (½″x¾″), 30cm (12″) long, can be nailed carefully along the front of each of the vertical dividers. Since the strips are about 19mm (¾″) wide they will cover the divider plus the gaps on either side. If there are no bothersome gaps then, of course, the strips are not necessary.

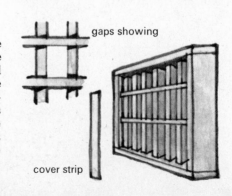

gaps showing

cover strip

The spice rack can either be left without any finish at all or an application of wax or polyurethane wood seal (matt finish) will protect the wood.

If you have any stick-on letters, labels or stencils, these can be used to label each compartment. After applying the labels cover them with a thin coat of clear matt polyurethane so that the letters don't come off when you clean the shelves.

The dimensions of the storage unit can be altered to make it suitable for holding cassettes and books. The addition of a backing board is optional.

Cassette storage unit

Another similar project, shown in the picture, can be built using the same surrounding border dimensions but with fewer grid pieces. It is easy to plan this by drawing the pieces and marking the dimensions clearly so that they are easy to follow.

You can add a thin plywood or hardboard backing piece. Your wood dealer will probably cut this accurately if you give the exact dimensions of the overall size of the box. This can be used to glue paper tiles to, either inside or outside. Plan the size of the grid for the particular tile or picture you are planning to use. Then simply nail the backing piece to the back of the assembled unit.

These ideas can be extended to cover a wide range of shelves and storage units depending on how ambitious you are. It would be easy to imagine a whole wall covered with these units, perhaps painted a bright red for the kitchen or white for the living-room. Then not only are the contents displayed but the shelf as well.

The rack can be placed on an existing shelf against a wall or you can fix brackets to the wall on which to rest it.

Chris Lewis

The art of enameling

Enamel 1

Enameling is a simple technique for making unique and practical decorative surfaces. Enameled finishes are colorful and hardwearing and can be used extensively in the home.

Enameling is an ancient craft dating back to the fifth century BC, when the Greeks used it with gold inlays. It is fundamentally colored glass, usually ground to a powder. This powder is spread on to a clean metal surface and

A beautiful example of enamel scrolling using a combination of transparent and opaque enamels. Designed by Richard Dent.

fired in a kiln at a temperature of about 750°C (1380°F). The powdered glass melts and fuses on the metal creating a hard, smooth surface. The brilliance of the colors used in enameling gives it its distinctive appearance, making it suitable for jewelry, small bowls, or ashtrays.

About enamels

Ready-made enamel powders of good quality save much time and effort in tedious grinding and are available in many good colors and varying quantities. It is not wise to mix different colors as you will probably get a speckled effect.

Once you have gained some experience you might want to grind your own enamel. Enamel in lump form—which has to be ground before use—has a longer shelf life than the powdered variety which tends to get mixed with dust and deteriorate. However, if you buy small quantities of ready-made powder which you then store in containers with tight-fitting lids you shouldn't have any difficulties.

Generally enamel powders melt at a temperature of around 750°C (1380°F) but there are some with a lower melting point which are sold as soft enamels. If a higher temperature is required they are termed hard enamels.

Types of enamel

Opaque enamels normally have a high gloss, smoothly textured finish, but different textures—such as a coarser, low gloss surface—can be obtained by leaving the piece in the kiln for a shorter period of time. This process is called underfiring.

Transparent enamels melt at a slightly higher temperature than the opaque enamels and are similar to colored glass in appearance. Transparent enamels must be fired on a clear, colorless enamel undercoat—called a flux—otherwise their color will be too concentrated. This is a slightly more involved technique than that of using the opaque enamels.

Transparent enamels cannot be underfired to vary their texture.

Different types of flux can be used to give different effects to the transparent colors fired on them.

Self-cracking enamel. This is a special variety of enamel powder that cracks or crazes like old porcelain. It is fired over an undercoat of whatever enamel you choose. Its textured surface looks old and interesting.

Metal blanks

The metal blanks are the bases used for firing the enamel on. Gold and silver provide the most reflective surface to use for transparent enamels. These are expensive so you might pre-

fer copper or gilding metal.

Copper is good to begin with as it fuses well with the different powders and it is fairly soft so that you can cut and shape your own blanks.

Dealers of enameling powders usually carry a wide range of metal blanks that are suitable to begin with. They are available in various shapes so that you can easily fire small test pieces before you embark on more ambitious projects.

A mica sheet blank can be used instead of a metal blank but the techniques involved are difficult and best left until you are familiar with the materials. The use of mica gives great depth to transparent work.

Kilns

The largest single item will be the kiln. Think carefully about what sort of work you want to do and what size kiln you will require.

The smallest kiln is suitable for pieces of jewelry but if you want to do larger pieces such as bowls and panels you will need a kiln with a larger muffle—ie the firing chamber. It is difficult to make more than one piece at a time, regardless of the size of the kiln, because of the amount of time and handling involved.

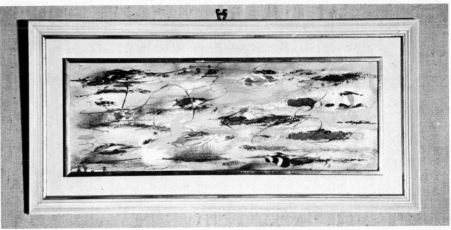

An impressionist wall panel fired in a large kiln. Designed by Richard Dent.

A kiln takes a while to warm up to the required temperature—the larger the muffle the longer it will take to reach the firing temperature.

Some kilns are equipped with heat regulators. This is useful if you are firing gold or silver, which have relatively low melting points, but if you are using copper or gilding metal you will learn after a few test pieces and some practice to recognize the bright orange of the firing chamber which indicates the correct temperature.

Technique

Blow torch. Small pieces can also be fired with a blow torch or a bunsen burner so if you have either of these you can try this method. Remember that the enamels must only get the heat from the flame and not be touched by the flame itself. A piece of metal held over the flame, with the enameled piece resting on it, will distribute the heat evenly. You will not be able to make large pieces with this method but you can make small pieces and combine them to form a larger piece by mounting them on a base.

These poppies illustrate what can be made with more advanced enameling techniques. Designed by Richard Dent.

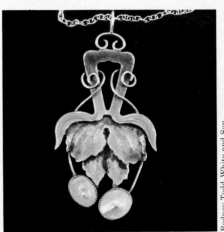

This beautiful pendant is typical of the high standard of enameling achieved during the Art Nouveau period.

Rodney Todd-White and Son

Basic tools

Tools are largely a matter of choice and you can add to this list as you gain experience. However, there are some tools that you cannot do without.

Asbestos glove—although not always essential—particularly with modern kilns—it does protect your hands from the heat when opening and closing the kiln door or lid.

Long-handled, 2-pronged fork for lifting pieces of work in and out of the kiln. You could improvise with an old toasting fork.

Sieve for sifting the enamel powders on to the metal blank. It can be made of metal or plastic and should be quite small—a coffee sieve will do.

Emery or sandpaper to remove the firescale which forms on the uncovered metal surface during firing. The firescale is difficult to remove so ideally you should paint this surface with anti-scale liquid. This is optional but makes cleaning much easier.

Wire wool pads or abrasive sponges are also useful for cleaning and shining the metal.

Brass tongs or long-handled tweezers to grip the metal once it has been cleaned. You must not touch the metal with your fingers before firing as this will leave traces of grease on it.

Stainless steel wire mesh stand (made for enameling) to place the pieces on in the firing chamber.

Palette knife for lifting the metal pieces on to the wire mesh—you could use a kitchen spatula.

The working area

The working area does not have to be large but it is essential to have the kiln on a heat resistant surface, preferably an asbestos mat, and the surrounding area should be fairly uncluttered. Place another asbestos mat next to the kiln on which to put the hot pieces. Cover the surface on which you work with sheets of paper. It makes it easier to collect any spilled powders and to clean up afterward.

Do not work too close to the kiln as the heat it generates can make you uncomfortable.

Simple enameling

Before you actually make anything it is useful to fire a few test pieces to become familiar with the equipment and the materials. Make a record of firing times and results and also the color. The color of the fired enamel is not always the same as the color of the powder. This record will be useful as a reference when you want special ef-

The small round enamels are test pieces for color. The metal blanks used were made of copper and can be bought in varying sizes and shapes.